SONIA L

SEE YOURSELF *Beautiful,* SEE YOURSELF HAPPY

AN INVITATION TO DISCOVER WHO YOU WERE MEANT TO BE

WHITAKER
HOUSE

SEE YOURSELF BEAUTIFUL, SEE YOURSELF HAPPY
An Invitation to Discover Who You Were Meant to Be

sonialuna.org
www.facebook.com/psonialuna
twitter.com/PSonialuna
www.YouTube.com/pastorasonialuna

ISBN: 979-8-88769-049-0
eBook ISBN: 979-8-88769-050-6
Printed in the United States of America
© 2023 by Sonia Luna

Whitaker House
1030 Hunt Valley Circle
New Kensington, PA 15068
www.whitakerhouse.com

Library of Congress Cataloging-in-Publication Data (Pending)

1 2 3 4 5 6 7 8 9 10 11   **W**   30 29 28 27 26 25 24 23

DEDICATION

To my mother Mercedes,
who taught me everything,
but first and foremost,
how to be a daughter.

CONTENTS

Acknowledgments 7

Introduction: Nothing Happens by Chance 13

1. I Have an Identity 15

2. Do I See Myself as I Really Am? 25

3. What Affects Me Does Not Determine My Future 33

4. Origins 45

5. First, I'm a Daughter 59

6. Vessel of Honor 71

7. Destroying the Haute Couture 81

8. How and When Does the Right Person
   Come Along? 87

9. You Deserve a Healthy and Genuine Relationship 99

10. A Woman with Whom You Want to Live 109

11. Imperfect But Right Marriages 117

12. A Lifelong Covenant 131

13. The Miracle of Being a Mother 141

14. Identity and Children 153

15. Why Do I Serve God and People? 163

16. The Blessing of Interceding 173

Epilogue: Our Infinite Catalyst Known as God 179

Balance Questionnaire 185

About the Author 189

ACKNOWLEDGMENTS

Thank you...

To God for loving me despite my imperfections, for teaching me every day the blessings of being a woman, and for allowing me to be born into a family where I first learned to be a daughter.

To my husband Cash for inspiring me with love and patience to be better every day.

To my children Cashito, Juan Diego, and Ana Gabriela for their love, understanding, and support in everything I do and for challenging me to be a better mom and person.

To Vanessa Chacón for her guidance in the area of psychology.

To Anna, Victor, and Julia, who kindly opened their hearts to me, sharing their testimony and trusting that they will be able to inspire and bless many people with it.

To Alfonso Guido for editing this book, to "Teacher" Elmer García for the English translation, and to the people who were kind enough to read several chapters before its publication.

And, of course, to all women in search of an identity for whom this book can help them find their infinite catalyst.

Then God said, "Let Us make man in Our image,
according to Our likeness."
—Genesis 1:26

And God made me a woman,
with long hair,
the eyes,
nose and mouth of a woman.

With curves
and folds
and soft hollows
and it dug me inside,
it made me a workshop of human beings.

Delicately weaved my nerves
and carefully balanced
the number of my hormones.
He composed my blood
and injected me with it
so that it irrigated
my whole body;
This is how ideas,
dreams,
instinct were born.

Everything that she gently created
with blows
and drills of love,
the thousand and one things that make me a woman
every day
for which I wake up proud
every morning
and bless my sex.

—Nicaraguan poet Gioconda Belli

INTRODUCTION:
NOTHING HAPPENS BY CHANCE

In every event in life, no matter how insignificant it may seem, God's will is implicit. For example, not taking a train and waiting for the next one; jotting down a phone number on a napkin; bidding farewell to a beloved family member forever; giving our first kiss to Juan and not to Eduardo; going to the supermarket and forgetting to get the cheese; going to the beach for the weekend and not the mountains; or attending a spiritual retreat and not a rock concert—everything has a reason for being.

Years ago, I was invited to watch a national volleyball tournament. That afternoon, I could have gone for some ice cream with my friends instead, but in the end, I decided to go to the sports center. And so that day, unbeknownst to me, I met the man who would one day become my husband.

Another day, while working and cooking at home, I left my cell phone in the kitchen. When I went to retrieve it, I realized that the pressure cooker I had on the stove was not closed properly. If I hadn't gone back for the phone, perhaps an explosion in the kitchen that day could have led to an irreversible fear of using a pressure cooker.

That is just how God works in our lives, with our important decisions and even in things we overlook, both with the transcendent and the mundane. And every event, no matter how insignificant it may seem, influences our identity, although it does not necessarily determine it. From choosing a blue dress because it is more appealing than a yellow one to realizing that we like psychology more than finances, from eating a mango and discovering that it is our favorite fruit to facing the passing of a sibling, everything that happens ends up shaping the person we are.

In this book, I embark on my life journey to explain how these *coincidences* have influenced my identity. Through personal anecdotes and real-life testimonies of other people, I'll attempt to show you the difference between the woman you are and the woman you see in yourself. I'll also explain the theory of how every person has many points of influence but just one *infinite catalyst* that marks them forever.

I genuinely hope that these pages will serve to build your life and help you discover your identity as a mother, an earthly daughter, a bride, a wife, a friend, and a daughter of God.

—Sonia Luna

1

I HAVE AN IDENTITY

The *Royal Spanish Academy Dictionary* defines the word *identity* as a "set of traits of an individual or a group that sets them apart from others." Another meaning states that it's "a consciousness that a person or group of people have of being themselves and different from others." The truth is that there are many attributes, both physical and abstract, that give us a unique identity.

For example, in my case, I am a brunette who does not like to eat seafood, although ironically, I enjoy cooking it.

Being a pastor, allergic to ginger, a woman, a Guatemalan, a victim of bullying in school, a volleyball player, someone who loves

It's not just my qualities
that make me someone but
also my flaws.

fashion designing, children, and exercising, and has a phobia of mice—all of these come together to make me *someone*. And simply crying while watching a movie with a sad ending also makes me unique.

However, it's not just my qualities that make me who I am but also my flaws. When I was a child, I used to bite my nails. When I was a teenager, I struggled with anger management. I am very absentminded when I have more work on my plate, and I have the inexplicable habit of rubbing my lips with my knuckles. Do you think I know why I do it? Well, honestly, I haven't the faintest idea. I just do it.

I have a friend who doesn't eat meat, which makes her a vegetarian, but beyond that, it is just one of many qualities that make up her identity. My husband had no siblings, but he was always very friendly to others, which also defines his identity. I had a father who suffered from alcoholism, but he was hardworking and very loving with his children, which also defined his identity.

All these qualities and flaws, be they physical, psychological, or even emotional, turn us into *someone* and make and define who we are. Every person possesses thousands of features that make them unique and let them know who they are. We can call this wide collection of qualities our *identity*.

There may be over 16 million Guatemalans, but not all are women, brunettes, pastors, or have a mouse phobia, nor are they all named Sonia Luna. And even if there were women in the world with these same characteristics, I can assure you that none of them would rub their lips with the knuckle of a finger on their right hand. We are all truly unique.

However, even though our identity makes us different, it can never define us. While it is true that there are some characteristics and events that can mark us forever—in my case, the bullying I suffered at school and the untimely death of one of my siblings—we all possess the ability to overcome these emotional hurdles.

Our identity is not a state we are born into and live with all our lives until our demise. Instead, it is shaped over time through people and events that define us. I emphasize people because we are all social beings. Our parents, siblings, school friends, coworkers, clients, teachers, and bosses are all part of our environment and exert significant influence on our identity. But while they may *influence* who we are, that is not to say that they can *determine* who we are. Our identity is fashioned over time through defining people and insights all around us.

AN INFINITE CATALYST

No one has a fixed identity. An eight-year-old child who is afraid of the dark might still be fearful when he's thirty unless he has overcome that and it no longer influences his identity.

Similarly, if a young girl smokes pot at age eighteen, that doesn't mean she's destined to smoke it her entire life. Nor does it mean that she will never graduate from college, have a steady job, or marry a good man.

What I am trying to say is that we all have the power to change our identity if we just discover what I have come to refer to as an *infinite catalyst*.

In life, we will have people, events, qualities, and shortcomings that influence our identity, of course. Still, the only thing that can determine it is a catalyst, either good or bad, the meaning that life has for us that marks us forever. Hence, the reason why it is infinite.

God is the reason why I pray
every day, why I consciously
try to abstain from sin,
and why I love to intercede
for people.

It becomes a watermark that defines us as soon as it occurs and turns into the essence of our identity. This is why I uphold the theory that all people discover and maintain an *infinite catalyst* throughout their lives that not only influences them but also defines them.

IDENTITY DIAGRAM

Qualities
Flaws
Life circumstances
Persons around us

} Influence us but don't define us

Infinite catalyst

} Gives us meaning and defines us

} All of this makes us someone and gives us an identity.

Let's just look for a moment at specific historical cases. We can assume that Ludwig van Beethoven's identity was strongly influenced by his admiration of Mozart, his relentless pursuit of perfection, his financial difficulties, and even his deafness. Still, his *infinite catalyst* was music. It motivated him to get up every morning, sit at the piano, and compose symphonies.

Likewise, Mother Teresa of Calcutta may have been influenced by her religious vocation, her mission in India, and even the Nobel Peace Prize she received in 1979, but her infinite catalyst was her humanitarian work. It drove her out into the streets to reach the poorest of the poor rather than remain inside a convent.

The identity of the Argentinean soccer player Lionel Messi may have been influenced by his friends in the city of Rosario in Argentina, his maternal grandmother to whom he dedicates every goal he scores, the genetic condition that kept him from growing normally, and even by his talent scout who took him to Spain, but in the end, his infinite catalyst was soccer. It is what motivates him to live a healthy lifestyle and train practically every day of his life.

These cases that I submit to you are a product of my perception. Still, the truth is that only you can discover the infinite catalyst that determines your identity forever. Do not forget that it is not an isolated fact but perpetual because of its infinite nature. Nor is it a quality, a flaw, or an essential person in your life because although they might all exert influence on your identity, they do not determine it.

An infinite catalyst is a sense of life that becomes the driving force of our fundamental actions and shifts something beyond our perception of reality. An infinite catalyst transforms our life entirely. And throughout this book, I will share how I discovered mine.

From an early age, I liked haute couture and wanted to be a fashion designer; however, although it influenced my way of looking at life, it was not what ultimately defined me. I also played volleyball during my teenage years and loved it, but it was not something that marked my life either. What about my family and children? They certainly are important and influential, but I had already experienced my *infinite catalyst* long before they came along. "So, Sonia," you may ask, "what was your infinite catalyst?"

My infinite catalyst was God and His consolation. It has led me to have a personal encounter with Him every day of my life and to think and act in a way that is consistent with His love. If God had not manifested Himself in my life, I would certainly not be Sonia Luna, an imperfect woman who has codirected a Christian ministry in Guatemala with her husband for over two decades. Nor perhaps would I be a wife who has been married over thirty-six years and believed that by marrying in a church, God could bless us. Without God manifesting Himself in my life, it's unlikely that I would have become the mother of three children who love Him.

God is the infinite catalyst that gives meaning to my days. He is the reason why I get up early every Sunday morning, shower, and get ready for church instead of staying at home in my pajamas, watching reruns of TV shows (no matter how much I get caught up in them), or playing golf or volleyball. Once I first experienced my *infinite catalyst*, I also accepted that Sunday is the day of the Lord.

God is also the reason why I pray every day, why I consciously try to abstain from sin, and why I love to intercede for people. In short, He has influenced every decision I make in life. As you can see, more than just an influence, He was my *infinite catalyst* and the One who made me who I am for all eternity.

And what about you? Have you discovered your infinite catalyst? My desire, throughout this book, is to help you discover it.

QUESTIONS FOR REFLECTION

1. What factors do you think influence your identity?

_____

_____

_____

_____

_____

2. What gives meaning to your life that might help you deter-
    mine your identity?

_____

_____

_____

_____

_____

2

DO I SEE MYSELF AS I REALLY AM?

Regardless of your age, by this point in life, you might already be aware that you are somebody and might even have discovered your infinite catalyst. Even so, you might still be looking at yourself incorrectly.

In other words, you may know that you are somebody without recognizing who you really are.

As beings created in the image and likeness of God, we have a body, a soul, and a spirit. Our nature is pure and perfect; it is also in constant motion. You find a common trend in everything you see. Plants hibernate in the winter and then bloom in the spring.

Just as everything around
you makes you someone,
it can also alter your
perception of who
you really are.

Some bird species migrate in search of food. In their natural habitat, mammals tend to live together in groups, and in practically the entire animal kingdom, mothers protect and feed their young.

As you can see, this entire perfect model also applies to us as human beings. While it is true that we have a special status because we are created in the image and likeness of God, our natural environment also teaches us in many ways about who we are and how we should conduct ourselves in life. We are blessed because we are rational beings, so we must not act as if we are not.

This is the reason why, as a woman who considers herself a child of God—and even more so, a person who is aware of how nature works—I find it difficult to understand some unnatural behaviors such as abortion, same-sex relationships, or the tendency to self-destruct through excessive alcohol or other substances. It is something that not only goes against my Christian principles but also against my way of looking at nature, especially in light of the fact that, unlike other species, human beings can reason and feel.

Evolutionary psychology asserts that there are four essential differences between our cognitive system and that of animals:

1. Our ability to combine different types of knowledge, data, and information, which can then be used to create, record, and transmit new knowledge.

2. Our ability to apply knowledge to problems and solutions in one situation or another.

3. Our ability to create and attend to symbolic representations using all our senses.

4. Our ability to establish a thought according to the information collected by our senses.

Something that prevents us
from discovering our infinite
catalyst is the
psychological and emotional
wounds that, over time, can
lead to deep traumas.

Human beings are adaptable to different types of situations, always based on our knowledge and reasoning. However, I will not stop loving someone no matter how unnatural their behavior may be because loving other people as we love ourselves is one of Jesus's commandments. (See Luke 10:27.) Nor will I try to persuade them to behave in one way or another. All I am trying to do in this book is show that we might often be misguided and have a self-perception of being someone that we are not, which is likely influenced by our environment or surroundings.

Ironically, our ability as human beings to reason can also become a particular disadvantage concerning other species. As beings with the ability to reason, it is undeniable that sooner or later, the day will come when we begin to question our very own existence: Who are we? Why are we here? What is our purpose? Why is there evil in the world?

It is not wrong to ask ourselves these kinds of questions, but they are also questions that, in one way or another, riddle us with doubts and fears that are typical of every human being. Until we discover the infinite catalyst that reveals our identity, these types of questions, rather than guide us toward truth, can end up confusing us.

Over time, psychological and emotional wounds can lead to deep traumas that also prevent us from discovering our infinite catalyst. Have you ever heard the phrase, "Though a wound may heal, the scar always remains"? This refers to wounds that we try to ignore as if they never happened, but deep in our consciousness, they remain.

An example of this is the criticism or taunts we may have been subjected to during childhood concerning our physical appearance, health, or even our gifts and talents. This happened to Jesus, who was criticized and discredited for teaching the Scriptures since he was just a Nazarene and the son of a carpenter. (See Matthew 13:55–58.)

My husband and I use the saying, "People are what they think of themselves." It is not something we made up, but something we have paraphrased from the Bible. Referring to every human being, Proverbs 23:7 says, *"For as he thinks in his heart, so is he."*

This reminds me of a testimony of self-love that a friend and a spiritual leader shared with me a long time ago. I just want to make a quick side note on the power of a testimony.

The first time I stepped foot on a pulpit was to testify what my life was like before and after I came to know God and discovered my *infinite catalyst*. A testimony is a firsthand account of someone who bears witness about an event, occurrence, or time they have experienced. It is not an exclusively spiritual tool, but it is also used in the media, criminal law, and even literature.

In the religious realm, a testimony helps us show the truthfulness of God's power and how significant He can be in our lives. And that is precisely what I shared that Sunday morning in 2001 when I first stepped onto a pulpit. I shared my testimony about how God had become my infinite catalyst through a series of specific events that I will get into in the following chapters.

One of the women who heard my testimony identified with it to such an extent that she wanted to share hers with me. In the next chapter, I will share it with you. As with other testimonies throughout this book, I have changed her name out of respect for her privacy. I hope Anna's story shows you how a person can be transformed when they encounter God and convinces you that nothing whatsoever is impossible for Him. (See Luke 1:37.) I also hope that it will illustrate how self-perception is key to healing any wound.

QUESTIONS FOR REFLECTION

1. If you had the opportunity, do you have a testimony that you would like to share with others?

_____

_____

_____

_____

_____

2. Do you recall any testimony that made a lasting impression on you?

_____

_____

_____

_____

_____

3

WHAT AFFECTS ME DOES NOT DETERMINE MY FUTURE

Anna recalls very little of her childhood. At the age of three, she suffered an accident that forced her to remain hospitalized for a year due to three skull fractures and greatly affected her motor skills.

However, Anna's wounds did not start with that accident. Rather, they began to manifest many years before her birth. Anna's mother was orphaned at the age of six and became pregnant with her first child at thirteen. This early pregnancy was the first of eight she had from different fathers, giving birth to six girls and two boys. Due to this situation, Anna's life was spent among seven stepfathers, two of whom constantly abused her and her sisters. In addition, Anna never knew who her birth father was.

Anna's mother became a prostitute to feed her children. Anna has never forgotten how her mother would come home drunk every night with some money to buy food for her children, which her older brother would administer despite the fact that he was not even yet of age.

All Anna ever received from her mother was physical, psychological, and verbal abuse. She became used to hearing phrases such as, "You are the ugliest of my daughters," "You are no good for anything," "You are useless," and "After the accident, you were left mentally retarded." Anna also remembers all of the shabby clothes and shoes that were given to her. She had to accept that reality, period.

Anna grew up believing that she did not deserve any better. After her accident at the age of three, she was left with certain problems that she did not fully understand, making her feel inferior to her siblings and everyone else. Her family believed this to be so true that her mother pulled her out of school, thinking she was not fit even for primary education.

FEELINGS OF UNWORTHINESS

By this point, Anna's identity clung to the idea of being inferior and unworthy because of her accident. She spent her entire childhood and part of her adolescence believing that she didn't even deserve to dream, causing her to grow up insecure, feeling like she had no allies, fearing adults, and certain that she couldn't count on anyone.

This could easily have been Anna's lifelong fate, but God had a great purpose for her.

Even with a sad start in life,
God had a great
purpose for Anna.

At the age of twelve, with the help of a neighbor, Anna decided to leave her home and seek shelter in a children's home. It was here that she discovered that she was not so useless after all, as she had the opportunity to learn various trades, including baking, cooking, and hair styling. After Anna had spent four years in the home, a woman "adopted" her to take her home to work as a domestic worker in exchange for paying for her studies—an agreement she never fulfilled. Instead, Anna was sexually assaulted by the woman's husband.

Anna returned to the children's home, begging to be taken back, but because she was then seventeen, she could no longer be accepted. However, a lady who had cared for her in the institution had pity on her and took her into her own home. During the week, Anna studied, and thanks to some strict social workers, she learned good manners, makeup tips, and other useful skills, turning her into a young lady.

Sometime later, Anna began to rebel. One day, she broke away from the care of these social workers and started living on her own. While living alone, she met an older friend who turned out to be a pimp who provided young escorts for wealthy men. Thus, Anna, for the first time in her life, began to rub shoulders with people of other levels of society. She also started drinking alcohol and keeping bad company.

After each party, she felt very lonely, empty, and worthless. No matter how much water she used to bathe, it was never enough to clean the filthiness that she felt inside. With no certain direction, Anna felt she had nothing to lose by taking her own life, so one day, she took a large quantity of pills. It was her fourth suicide attempt. She ended up in a hospital to have the contents of her stomach pumped out. While still in recovery, she called a friend who assured her, "Bad times can be fixed with good times." Her friend arranged a date with two other guys. That evening, Anna danced with Luis, drank, and ended up in the bathroom crying. She spent the night with Luis and that's where she woke up the following morning.

PRAYING FOR DELIVERANCE

Anna returned home stricken, riddled with shame, and with that same feeling of emptiness. It was then that she prayed, "Lord, if You deliver me out of this, I will understand that it isn't what You want for my life." She did not know any other lifestyle than the one she was living, the only one that was consistent with her perception of herself. Her only hope was for God to do something in her life.

Moments later, Luis, an estranged Christian, knocked on her door, concerned about her health and condition. That day, Anna told him a lot about her life. Feeling moved by her sad experiences, Luis told her about Jesus. "You know," he said, "Jesus Christ died for you, so that you don't have to live that life. In Him, your life can be made new." Luis was also going through a rough patch, but nothing would keep him from talking to Anna about a new opportunity. Without giving it a second thought, after a drunken binge and in the middle of a hangover, Anna said yes to Jesus.

Anna and Luis fell in love and began to change their bad habits. They went to church together, and Anna attended her first encounter retreat. When she heard the preacher talking about generational curses such as single motherhood, alcoholism, prostitution, and divorce, she understood that she did not have to make all of those bondages her identity—she could be free of them. She then said a prayer to break and renounce all of those curses. For the first time in her life, she truly felt free and hopeful.

Anna continued her relationship with Luis, although from the moment they started dating, it was clear that he would never marry her. So one month after going steady, he decided to leave her. He could not get over the circumstances by which he and Anna had met. He was looking for a bride to marry, but he wanted a woman without a past as tumultuous as hers. He had decided to break up with Anna, but by then, she was already pregnant with their first daughter. Luis even doubted if the baby was really his, but once the child was born, the resemblance was so uncanny that he went on visiting Anna without ever committing to her.

The relationship between the two became violent. She prayed once again, saying, "Lord, I renounced all those generational curses, and You promised that my offspring would not have to live what I went through. I ask You to have Luis acknowledge his daughter." Then she heard Jesus speak to her heart and say, "I always keep my promises."

PROMISES FULFILLED

Six months later, Luis sought her out and acknowledged his daughter. He reconciled with Anna, but he still wasn't convinced that he should marry her and had no qualms about letting her know that. He rented an apartment for her and visited her on some weekends, but he still did not want to commit.

She became pregnant with their second daughter, and the news was not well received by Luis or his family. However, he continued to visit her, unable to forget her past. Some time later, Anna became pregnant for the third time with a child that was never born, as she decided to have an abortion. She almost bled to death from the procedure.

Once again, Anna sank into a deep depression. It seemed as if life was bent on denying her happiness, and she began to doubt her purpose again. In sharing her testimony, she said, "On the one hand, you have the malice within people, and on the other hand, God was still not answering me." Finally, one day, she said to herself, "I'm just going to disappear. I will leave my daughters with their father and let him take care of them. I can't do this anymore." Anna had given up. Her dreams were shattered, and she continually thought of suicide. It was clear that Luis was still looking for the woman of his dreams, and it was not her.

But God had other plans.

Three years after the birth of their first daughter, Luis came for a visit and brought them some groceries from the supermarket. As Anna began to place them in the pantry, she saw a jewelry box inside one of the bags. She told Luis, "You need to return this. Someone put it in here by mistake." That's when Luis walked up to her, opened the box, showed her the ring, and asked her to marry him.

Later, Luis told her about a moment he had with God. He said the Lord told him, "The wife you have always been looking for is Anna. If you reject her again, you will never have the wife you asked me for." Only then did Luis find peace in his heart and do away with every hesitation he had about Anna.

Mistreatment, rejection, and abuse conspired to change Anna's identity, but she understood that the road she traveled on was not as important as her final destination. Her stepfather predicted that she would become a prostitute, her mother told her that she was useless, and the world challenged her with so many temptations that she had hit rock bottom by the age of eighteen. No one could foresee that God had a future so full of hope in store for her! He healed her, cleansed her, and fulfilled His promises to her.

Anna and Luis have now been married for twenty years. She is happy to be the wife of a wonderful man who God used to shape

No matter how unique, different, or stormy our experiences may be, there is absolutely no life on the earth that cannot be transformed by God.

her faith. Luis inspires her to serve God every day, always encouraging her to share her testimony with those who need to find their true identity.

Anna is an entrepreneur in her city and pastors a church together with Luis. They had a third child, a son, and already have two grandchildren. Her story can be perfectly seen in the following Bible passage from Romans 8:37–39:

> Yet in all these things we are more than conquerors through Him who loved us. For I am persuaded that neither death nor life, nor angels nor principalities nor powers, nor things present nor things to come, nor height nor depth, nor any other created thing, shall be able to separate us from the love of God which is in Christ Jesus our Lord.

I can draw some conclusions from Anna's testimony, and I would like to invite you to reflect on them and also draw your own.

First of all, there were different things that kept her from discovering her identity. She was destined to suffer even before she was born, affected not only by her early childhood environment, but also by the consequences of her own actions.

Second, these issues started manifesting throughout her life and do not correspond to a single stage. We can see that once Anna thought she had discovered love, she crashed head-on into a wall of disappointment that almost drove her to suicide. Her experience proves that there is no right age at which to discover our identity. As is often the case, once we think we have come to know for sure who we are and where we are going, something changes. Life is full of surprises.

Third, no matter how unique, different, or stormy our experiences may be, there is absolutely no life on the earth that cannot be transformed by God. Anna's life is just one of many examples.

What conclusions can you draw from Anna's testimony? What conclusions can you draw from your own testimony? If you have something to share, I urge you to approach the people you trust the most and share what you have in your heart.

If you still don't feel confident about doing so, I encourage you to write it down. Take a notebook and write your own life story. Perhaps you might find out that many of the things you jot down are the ones keeping you from discovering your true identity as a child of God.

QUESTIONS FOR REFLECTION

1. What events in life have affected you so much that you have questioned who you are?

   _____

   _____

   _____

   _____

   _____

2. Have you recovered from these or do you feel that some of them are keeping you from discovering your true identity?

   _____

   _____

   _____

   _____

   _____

4

ORIGINS

My name is Sonia María Castillo Pacheco, and I was born in Guatemala City on May 19, 1966. But ever since I was a young child, my family lived in the interior of the country. In the 1970s, we lived in a region of Guatemala known as Retalhuleu, which is made up of nine townships and whose capital city is located 190 kilometers from Guatemala City. The city of Retalhuleu is described by its inhabitants as "the capital of the world," and its name means "Sign made on the earth."

My father Jaime and my mother María Mercedes had five children: two sons and three daughters—Jaime; Oscar Francisco or Calin; Diana; Sonia Maria (me); and Barbara. I was born when

Diana was eight years old, and Barbara was born when I was nine years old. Because of these age gaps, I connected more with my brothers than my sisters.

When I was young, there were many cotton and banana plantations in Retalhuleu. We moved there because my father was a crop duster. Prior to this, he had worked in the control tower of Guatemala City's La Aurora International Airport. Later, my father studied at the aviation academy so that he could become a pilot.

My two brothers followed in his footsteps, also studying to become pilots. Although my older sister wanted to do so as well, my father never allowed it, arguing that it was not an ideal profession for a woman. I honestly don't know my father's true reasons for denying her the opportunity to become a pilot. Being overprotective of women has always been a part of the Latin American culture. I know there is a lot to be said on this subject, but sometimes, I'm led to believe that this situation may have influenced my sister's identity.

As children, we used to play games with friends and neighbors in our garden, which was filled with mango, tangerine, and lemon trees. There was also an airplane frame that our father set up for us to play in.

In the home to the right of ours lived the family of Jorge and Dinora Jacobs, whose children were my classmates and became my best friends at the time. Our neighbors to the left included the family of Ricardo Alejos, who was known for his social work. On the other side of the street lived Carmencita, a friend with whom I spent many afternoons after school.

My mother studied to become a teacher, but she never worked as one; instead, she developed her other talents to help with the family income. In addition to being a great cook, she also made clothes and owned a beauty salon. There was a large table in our home that she used to make tailoring cuts for her clients' dresses and miniature wedding dresses for the dolls that decorated wedding cakes. Working from home enabled my mother to care for us, make meals for us, and educate us.

However, our home was not always a happy one. Although my father was a hardworking, responsible man, he was also a victim of alcoholism and disappeared for days on drunken binges. This caused a lot of tension between him and my mother. Many times, my siblings and I had to intervene to keep them from hurting each other.

I recall one night in particular when my parents got into such a loud, heated argument in our backyard that my mom took my dad's gun and pointed it straight at him. I had to snatch the gun from her and then run, crying, to our neighbors' house to ask for help.

Between the ages of eight and fourteen, I witnessed the worst marital crisis my parents ever had, with my father's alcoholism taking a direct toll on our family's finances. And just when I thought that things were starting to get back to normal in our lives, my mother felt the urge to return to Guatemala City. By then, I was about to turn fifteen.

In Latin America, a girl's *quinceañera* is usually a big celebration for her fifteenth birthday because it marks the stage when she becomes a young lady. The word comes from two Spanish words: *quince* (fifteen) and *años* (year). It is an exciting occasion for the sweet fifteen birthday girl, who wears a long, elegant dress that day. Without generalizing, I'm sure that most girls of my generation dreamed of that event, and I was certainly not the exception.

However, my mom decided that the best quinceañera gift for me would not be a party, but a trip to the United States to study

The development of our identity is a long and complex process that occurs throughout our lives.

and perfect my English. I understood what she was recommending and accepted it without objection, knowing that it was the best thing for me. I have met very few women from her generation as visionary and ahead of their time as she was. From a very young age, I felt grateful for the trust she placed in me.

Upon returning from the U.S., I heard the wonderful news that my dad had quit drinking and was going to church. God alone could have saved my parents' marriage by bringing about a miraculous and radical change in his life.

I am frequently asked, "When does our identity begin to form?" As I mentioned earlier, there is no specific moment. The development of our identity is a long and complex process that we experience throughout our lives. We begin to experience it during early childhood, but it really starts long before we are born.

GENERATIONAL LINKS AND CONFLICTS

Entire generations in a family can be marked by either healthy or conflicting relationships. In the Old Testament, we see that the blessing that Abraham gave Isaac also influenced his offspring; however, the conflicts between his wife Sarah and her maid Hagar led to a separation between their children. When Sarah's son Isaac was weaned at age two or three, Hagar's son Ishmael, then sixteen or seventeen, made fun of his half-brother. (See Genesis 21:9.) Thus over the years, there have been wars and conflicts between Jews, Isaac's descendants, and Arabs, Ishmael's descendants.

In the same way, we see how the conflict over progeny— and Rebekah's preference for that birthright—caused the twin brothers Jacob and Esau to drift apart. The rejection and betrayal that Esau felt caused a root of bitterness to emerge, so that he came to hate his brother and wanted him dead. (See Genesis 27:41.)

There was also the deception of Laban, Jacob's father-in-law. Laban gave Leah to Jacob as a wife, knowing that he loved Rachel. This led him to love Rachel's sons (Joseph and Benjamin) more than Leah's sons and their daughters. This stoked jealousy, anger, and envy in Jacob's other sons, as well as the desire to kill their brother Joseph because of the preference that their father bestowed on him.

As a result, Joseph suffered not only his brothers' rejection, but also the worst of betrayals: they humiliated him by taking away the tunic of many colors his father had made for him and cast him into a pit, planning to kill him. Instead, they sold Joseph into slavery to the Ishmaelites for twenty pieces of silver. (See Genesis 37:23–28.) Joseph went through many trials before he finally saw his family again.

However, we can clearly see how God rescues us and makes all things work together to bless us. And although it seemed that everything Joseph went through would be detrimental to his purpose, in reality, every dream God had for him and his people was fulfilled. (See Genesis 45:3–8.)

Satan tried to sabotage the blessing on Joseph's life with the wounds caused by his brothers, but God allowed Joseph to reconcile with his entire family, forgive, and heal his heart, so that his father had the opportunity to bless his grandsons Manasseh and Ephraim. (See Genesis 48:12–14.)

EXAMINING RELATIONSHIPS WITH A GENOGRAM

As an adult, I had the opportunity to do a little more research about why my parents had such a conflictive relationship, and why other members of my family with direct relationships—such as adult relatives and their children—didn't end up with the same behavioral patterns. That is when I discovered the genogram, a tool used in psychology to study family relationships.

I spent a lot of time trying to draw my family's genogram. This helped me understand how we can inherit behaviors, including those that come from generations before our parents, which is what happened to my dad.

GENOGRAM KEY
Types of Family Relationships

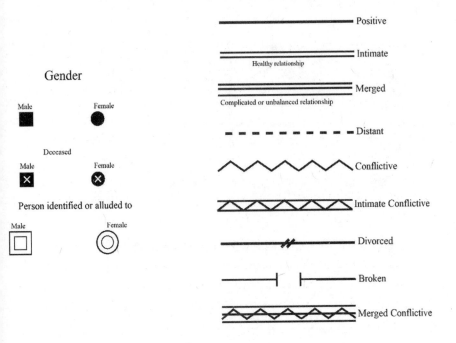

I would like to share my genogram with you and invite you to create your own. You can find many tools on the Internet to help you do this.

Sonia Luna's Genogram

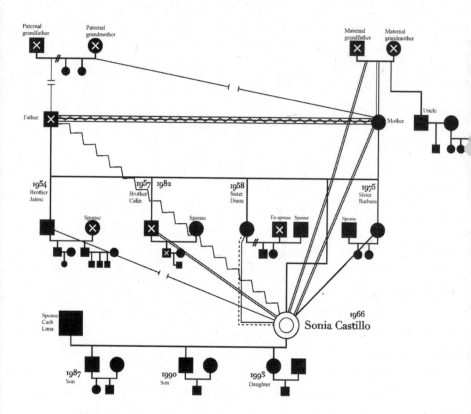

CHILDHOOD COMPLEXES AND BULLYING

When I was a child, my parents never made any remarks comparing my siblings and me. They always gave me their affection, and it boosted my self-confidence. However, I did make the mistake of comparing myself to my older sister Diana, who was very pretty compared to me and a model, which I also wanted to be.

I got along well with all of my siblings. We always joked and laughed, but each one's way of doing so was different. I was especially affected by Diana's remarks because every time she was

Despite the bullying I endured at school, the presence of my parents helped me to be emotionally stable.

angry with me, she would tell me that my parents had found me "on the street."

This type of bullying not only took place at home but also at school, where it was worse. Many times, I have shared that I was chubby as a child. As if that were not enough, I had to take antibiotics for tonsillitis, which caused the enamel on my teeth to become darker. So despite the love I received at home, I went through issues regarding my identity when my classmates called me nicknames and made fun of my body shape. It was the first time I became aware of what it was like to feel bad about yourself because of your appearance.

What we now call *bullying* didn't really have a name when I was a child, but it has been around forever. If you have suffered this kind of psychological abuse, don't think it's something new. Even if they don't tell you about it, it's likely that your parents and grandparents were exposed to it too.

In my case, the abuse took a toll on me without my realizing it and in such a way that I began to believe that I would always be the same. Back then, I didn't know what a complex was, nor that I could be developing a wrong image of myself.

Even so, I always tried to excel at school. Although I suffered from the way people looked at me, I tried to keep that sadness to myself and not show it—although many years later, I realized it had taken an emotional toll on my health. I was never spiteful but rather quite friendly. I remember going to the river a lot, target shooting, playing ball, and in general engaging in unusual activities for girls my age, pastimes that were usually only done by boys.

Throughout this entire process, my parents always looked out for me. They would always check on me, asking how I was doing in school and who my friends were. My mom always attended every school activity. She never sent anyone else to pick up my grades and motivated me to play sports, learn different languages, and engage in extracurricular activities. Despite the bullying I endured at school, the presence of my parents helped me to be emotionally stable. My mom and I always maintained a close communication. She taught me manners, the importance of following rules, self-discipline, and, above all, to value myself as a woman.

If you are going through a season of bullying:

+ Don't try to handle it on your own. The role of your parents or a close relative is crucial to externalize what is happening to you. They will provide you with all of the encouragement and reassurance you need at this time. My mother was instrumental when I went through this ordeal.

+ Don't remain silent. Report the problem to your teachers or school authorities so they can take the necessary action.

+ Don't exact revenge. The worst thing you can do is lower yourself to the level of your aggressors and take justice into your own hands. Leave it to the proper authorities to administer justice.

If you are the mother of a child who is going through this type of distress:

+ Even if at first glance there are no signs of bullying, always monitor your child's state of mind and keep an eye on his or her environment. Get more involved but be careful to respect your child's privacy.

+ In no way normalize the problem or downplay its importance, but at the same time, do not dramatize the situation or make your child feel ashamed or embarrassed by it. Let them know that no matter what happens, you are on their side, and that the problem is something you can work out together with the right communication.

+ Encourage positive thinking and work on their communication skills so that their self-esteem, emotional intelligence, and assertiveness grow, and the child or adolescent learns to express their opinions and emotions correctly.

+ Go to their school and seriously expose the gravity of the matter. However, keep your temper in check and make sure that you do not embarrass your son or daughter in front of his or her classmates or school authorities. As much as possible, try to do this when your child is not present.

+ Encourage your child to keep their mind busy with extra-curricular activities such as team sports, theater, painting, music classes, or other pursuits so that he or she can develop new social relationships and discover other hobbies.

QUESTIONS FOR REFLECTION

1. Did you suffer bullying as a child, as a teenager, or are you
    perhaps suffering from it right now?

    _____

    _____

    _____

    _____

    _____

2. Have you been able to work through it or do you believe that
    much of your behavior or self-image is a result of those experi-
    ences? Do you understand that bullying affects or has affected
    your identity?

    _____

    _____

    _____

    _____

    _____

5

FIRST, I'M A DAUGHTER

Sometimes, it can seem mean-spirited to compare the present with past ages since each has its advantages and disadvantages. Still, in my youth, it was extremely rare to hear about girls or teen-agers who were married or sexually active. Sadly, that's no longer the case today.

According to a national census conducted in 2018, females comprise 52 percent of Guatemala's population. Of these, half are between the ages of one day old and twenty-four years old. Among those who are mothers, the average age at which they had their first child was nineteen years old. As you can see, so far, there is

A woman who feels loved
as a daughter, from the time
she is a child, has a greater
chance of safely performing
any other role in life, whether
it be that of a mother, wife,
leader, or professional.

nothing alarming in these statistics, except for this sad reality: six out of ten mothers are single.

These figures add to studies indicating that Latin America is the region with the highest number of children born out of wedlock—that is, single mothers. Women have their first child before the age of twenty. Turning to the United States, there are 1.19 million Hispanic families made up of single mothers.

I know that by this point, many might say, "Well, it doesn't matter because every woman can be self-sufficient." Of course, they can, but one must add much more alarming and discouraging data to these statistics. According to research published in Guatemala's national newspaper *Prensa Libre* (*Free Press*) on September 19, 2019, almost one million girls and adolescents in my country are mothers. And despite it being classified as a crime, the headline read, "There are 82,201 women in the country who had a child before the age of 15."

And there is more: under Guatemalan law, a person is of legal age once they turn eighteen, but engaging in sexual activity with a minor is only a crime if the minor is fourteen years old or younger. In other words, pedophilia is only partially criminalized by the law.

Regardless of whether they are protected under the law, it's important for girls to grow up in a healthy home environment where they can feel the great joy of being a daughter. Daughter first, then a woman. Daughter first, then a student. Daughter first, then a professional. Daughter first, then a girlfriend or a wife. Daughter first, then a mother. And I emphasize this because a woman who feels loved as a daughter, from the time she is a child, has a greater chance of safely performing any other role in life, whether it be that of a mother, wife, leader, or professional.

If a parent shows their daughter from a young age how valuable she is, she will remember and treasure it always, before any person or circumstance.

Of course, that is not to say that all other roles in life are not important because of course they are, and each one comes with its own challenges. But if you were to ask me, I will not hesitate in answering that I am first and foremost a daughter, then a wife, then a mother, and finally a professional. Even today—at fifty-four years old, almost thirty-six of them as a wife, after raising three children and now a grandmother—the predominant role in my identity is that of a daughter. It is something that defines who I am today. If a parent shows their daughter from a young age how valuable she is, she will remember and treasure it always, before any person or circumstance.

Now, I know that many people, both men and women alike, might have never had the opportunity to have a father or a mother. However, I want you to know that God is also our heavenly Father and loves us unconditionally. In Him, we can find more love than we could ever hope to receive in this world. His love is pure and honest because He sees us as we truly are and not as how we or anyone else may see us.

CHILDHOOD IN CONFRONTATION

All too often, we don't understand what is going on in our lives until we face that wounded child we once were. Remember that although I tried to reflect a personality filled with self-confidence to others as a child, I spent many years holding back negative things because of the teasing I received at school or the comparisons I put myself through with my older sister. In my view, these feelings were in the past, yet they still affected me.

A couple of years ago, I was having some digestive issues, and I visited a homeopathic doctor. It was a rather strange medical appointment. I recall that I had to make some last-minute

There's a famous saying in my homeland, "The pitcher goes to the well so often that it finally breaks."

arrangements for a flight abroad the following day, so I urgently asked the doctor to see me, even if it was over the phone.

However, she said no and made me come into her clinic, stating that she needed to see me and hear firsthand what was happening. Even though she knew it was urgent and it would be pretty tricky for me to get to her clinic, she was so insistent that I had no choice but to jump in the car and drive to her clinic in a hurry, at the risk of delaying my travel arrangements. But what do you think happened?

At a previous medical appointment with her, I had casually talked about many experiences I had had as a child, especially some childhood fears. So in my return visit to her clinic, she took out a blank sheet of paper and began to draw an iceberg, which she divided into two parts: one part that emerges on the surface and the other that remains underwater.

ICEBERG METAPHOR

The part of the iceberg that we can see is the smallest part of its actual size. Just like an iceberg, we show the world only 10 percent of who we are, represented by our consciousness and our rational behavior—in other words, everything we feel and live in the present. The additional 90 percent is hidden underwater and corresponds to our subconsciousness.

As the doctor continued to draw, I thought to myself, *How can this doctor want to give me—at this point of my life, as a woman loved by my inner circle, with a normal family and a stable job—a psychology class that I never asked for? All I want is something to get my digestion back in order!*

Nonetheless, I was patient to see what she wanted to tell me, until she said, "The pitcher goes to the well so often that it finally breaks." When I asked her what she meant with this typical Guatemalan saying, she replied that there are so many negative experiences that build up in our subconscious over the years—frustration, sadness, pain, anger, fear—that there comes a point when everything explodes and ends up damaging our health.

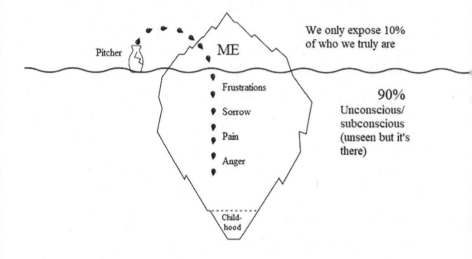

Although what she was telling me was quite interesting, it still didn't fix my digestive problems. However, her words got me thinking. After analyzing everything I had told her in our previous session, she revealed that much of what was currently affecting my physical health was due to an obsession I always had as a child to be a *savior.* "How so?" I asked.

The doctor continued, "The base of the iceberg corresponds to the subconsciousness of that child savior that you always wanted to be and still want to be today." This revelation had such an impact on me that I was no longer worried about the time or the trip the following day. The doctor explained that assuming this role of savior meant that, rather than facing my own problems, I worked to protect others from theirs. This made a lot of sense as I recalled my childhood days when, despite being one of the younger siblings, I always looked out for my parents' well-being, not only individually but also in their marriage.

"Your digestive issues are due to your problem with managing emotions," she continued. "What is affecting you so much, Sonia?" I was about to say my digestive disorder, but before I could get a word in, she said, "Somehow, you still feel responsible for your dad's drinking problem and your brother's death. Furthermore, for a long time, you took on the role of a savior to restore your parents' marriage and bring them closer to God. And if that weren't enough, now your job is to pray and intercede for other people in need. Do you realize that, Sonia? You've spent your entire life wanting to save others instead of caring about yourself."

I was stunned. The doctor went on, "So you may find what I'm about to tell you strange, Sonia, but I'm definitely going to have to ask you to love yourself. Please balance your life." I asked her if that was all, and she said yes. Syrups, medication, rest? Nope, nothing else. She just told me to start balancing my life from the moment I stepped foot out of her clinic.

I left there feeling very confronted. I realized that the doctor might be on to something. So as soon as I got back home, I began to research the subject in-depth, reading medical articles and talking to friends who were specialists in psychology. That is how I discovered that I had tried to make up for the traumas I suffered as a child by protecting other people—despite my apparent security in front of everyone. And it wasn't until that moment that I discovered how I always felt unprotected despite the love I received from my family. One way or another, I spent my whole life seeking to compensate for that lack of protection with my obsession to protect others.

I concluded that I couldn't continue to take on a role that didn't belong to me. I even went so far as to ask myself, "How could you have been so stupid all this time?" I reminisced about many people and situations in my life related to work, my husband, pastors in the ministry, my children, and even my grandchildren. Perhaps, without diminishing the love I have for all of them, I realized that many times, I gave them my protection at the expense of my own well-being.

On the other hand, it also revealed how transcendental childhood is in anyone's life, whether you're a man or a woman. It made me see how far the side effects of a good or bad childhood can reach. But again, I embraced God's Word that says He can restore every area of our life because His strength is made perfect in our weakness. (See 2 Corinthians 12:9.)

QUESTIONS FOR REFLECTION

1. Do you recall incidents or conditions from your childhood that could be linked to any physical or emotional distress that you have?

_____

_____

_____

_____

_____

2. Have you thought how those circumstances might be affecting you now?

_____

_____

_____

_____

_____

6

VESSEL OF HONOR

During puberty, a human being's main biological, sexual, social, and psychological changes take place. According to the World Health Organization, adolescence covers the period between ages ten and nineteen, although some assert that it gradually enters adulthood, stretching out to age twenty-four. At this stage, an individual's social maturity begins to manifest, and different models of belonging and community are tested.

It was during this stage that my height grew, but I still struggled with being overweight. My mother always tried to make me feel comfortable with myself. She designed clothes that were well-suited to my figure and began to keep tabs on what I ate. Suddenly

It is only when we realize
how valuable we are to God
that we start noticing the
right or wrong concept we
have of ourselves.

my high-calorie diet was replaced with healthier foods. I also started playing sports, and because of my height, I was able to join the basketball and volleyball teams.

It was also during this time that I came to know God and accepted Christ as my personal Lord and Savior, an experience I will discuss a bit later. Everything started to make sense. It is only when we realize how valuable we are to God that we start noticing the right or wrong concept we have of ourselves.

Paul wrote:

For I say, through the grace given to me, to everyone who is among you, not to think of himself more highly than he ought to think, but to think soberly, as God has dealt to each one a measure of faith.   (Romans 12:3)

God always shows His love for all of His children, without exception, and He motivates us to do the same. Every time we are confused, we can always count on Him to show us a way out.

When a person has very low self-esteem, they are usually motivated to increase it. The same thing happens when they have a very high opinion of themselves; they are encouraged to be humble and find a balance. However, sometimes people do not have one or the other, and they need to be motivated to discover who they are for themselves and not have someone else tell them or make them believe they are someone that they are not.

By way of example, I would like to share Victor's testimony with you.

A VESSEL OF HONOR

Born in El Salvador, Victor had a quiet childhood, although he grew up in a dysfunctional home with three older half-brothers on his mother's side and a younger sister born to both of his parents.

His father would disappear for long periods of time because he worked far away and was also an alcoholic. Victor's mother caught him in many affairs until, one day, she finally decided to separate from him, go to work, and raise their children on her own. This left Victor and his sister without adult supervision for much of the time. Although they were financially deprived, they were happy in their own way, but Victor felt hurt by his father's rejection and abandonment.

His mother washed and ironed clothes for a family. Victor and his sister would anxiously wait for her to return home every day since she would bring them food in plastic bags—leftovers from the house where she worked. It was exciting for them to wait for the surprise menu.

As a teenager, Victor was very content with his life. He had no aspirations and did not see the world beyond his nose. Nor does Victor remember having any dreams. He was in a comfort zone and saw his life as something normal. However, he cared a lot about what his mother and others thought of him.

He was a very quiet boy with a slight, slim build. And although his friends urged him to smoke and drink, Victor always turned down these types of offers. He also did not like being told what to do and, as a result, began to be verbally and physically abused by his friends. Many times, the abuse would turn into severe beatings. Victor never tried to stand up for himself since he knew he could not achieve anything by doing so. In addition to being poor, he did not wear designer clothes or shoes or brand-name items like his friends did. This gave Victor an inferiority complex.

A HARDENED HEART

As time went by, Victor's heart hardened. He became defensive, and everyone noticed a significant change in his demeanor. He also felt an enormous need for revenge. He was going through puberty when one of his brother's friends began to harass him. He invited Victor to his house on one occasion, locked him up, and abused him sexually. Victor was twelve years old at the time.

This man threatened to tell Victor's mother if he said anything. Such was the abuse, possession, and control he exerted over Victor's mind that Victor became a puppet to fulfill his every desire. There was even an occasion when he not only satisfied him but several men in the same house. Victor started to feel very dirty and used. A feeling of resentment toward other people, especially toward men, began to grow inside him—along with a thirst for revenge.

As Victor grew older, he began to destroy dating relationships, getting involved even in relationships that seemed solid, all for the sole purpose of destroying marriages and ruining the reputation of the men he managed to attract. Victor felt a certain satisfaction in doing so. He donned a mask of insensitivity without ever thinking that the one who was ultimately being destroyed little by little was himself.

When he was a child, he always imagined that he would study hard in school, graduate, get a job, buy a house, and have a normal family. However, everything that transpired during his eight years of adolescence defined what he came to believe was his future. By that age, Victor had become submissive, fearful, and complacent, yet at the same time, his heart continued to harden. He was no longer able to empathize with anyone.

In addition, he became racist, classist, and proud. He started to wear nicer clothes, which aroused the interest of those around him. And although all of this had marred him, inside, Victor still asked himself, "Will I ever experience true love?" Until then, all of his relationships had been to fulfill the demands of others or to exact revenge. However, he longed to experience true love in a normal relationship.

After his mother died, Victor lived by himself for the first time and went to work as a hair stylist. He met new people and began to receive praise and recognition for his work. He was accepted just as he was, and people were drawn to his mysterious and daring image, which boosted his ego. For the first time, Victor had a dream to go somewhere else, start over from scratch, and improve professionally and financially.

GOD DRAWS NEAR

On one occasion, Victor heard a message from Pastor Cash Luna on a radio program. Curiously, he waited to hear the next program and continued to listen to Cash. It was then that Victor felt God intervening in his life for the very first time...but he soon forgot all about it.

Months went by. Then Victor received an invitation to work in Guatemala. With great enthusiasm, he decided to migrate and settle down. At this new workplace, he assisted many women— including me—as a stylist. He was surprised when I told him that I was Pastor Cash's wife.

One day, I invited Victor to attend our Hechos 29 annual youth conference at our church, Casa de Dios. Brimming with enthusiasm, he accepted, and God spoke to him there. Soon,

We are restored instruments
of God, filled with His Holy
Spirit, to fill those around us.

Victor came to know God as a loving Father and decided to start a new life, accepting Jesus into his heart.

Later, Victor met the woman who is now his wife at Casa de Dios. Their marriage has not been all that easy. He had to deal with the ghosts of his past. Although he had a good marriage, his thoughts often betrayed him. The situation was not easy for him and his wife, a sensible woman with the patience and wisdom to give Victor the time he needed to free himself of his past.

After thirteen years of marriage and two children, Victor received the devastating news that he was HIV positive. He knew that it was a consequence of his past, but today he knows that he has been given a new opportunity and is undergoing treatment. Victor found professional medical support from his doctors, but also the moral support from me, the church, and, above all, his wife.

A VESSEL FULL OF LOVE

At the time of this testimony, Victor sees himself as a vessel of mercy, like the vessels used in public squares that people can drink from after having been restored.

He grew up with a father who was unconcerned about what was happening to him and spent a lot of time filled with hatred and a desire for revenge. However, he now lives in gratitude to the Lord for being able to share testimonies of love and mercy like this one.

Victor admits that God has been with him at every stage of his life. Otherwise, he would not have endured all the hell he went through in his youth.

Victor affirms that he has now found true love. His wife loves, supports, and admires him. She has promised to be with him always. They have many years ahead of them, and for as long as they live, they will testify of the power of God as a family over-flowing in gratitude. As Victor says, they know that the Lord is a master at "turning the vilest thing into a vessel of honor."

The most important conclusion to draw from Victor's testi-mony is that, with God's help, we can all deal with the ghosts of our past and renew our thoughts.

That does not mean that our life is automatically resolved from the moment we come to know Jesus, nor does it mean that, sooner or later, we will not have to face the aftermath of our past. However, Christ will also give us the strength when we accept Him as our Lord and Savior. It is one thing to face a problem as a person who does not have Christ in his heart and quite another to face it as someone who sees Jesus as their Savior.

Furthermore, the fact that Victor has a righteous self-image and sees himself as a vessel of honor illustrates how valuable we are to contain even the most priceless liquid in the universe. We are restored instruments of God, filled with His Holy Spirit, to serve those around us.

QUESTIONS FOR REFLECTION

1. How have you noticed your self-image affecting your identity?

_____

_____

_____

_____

_____

2. When you read Victor's testimony, what do you feel that God can do with you?

_____

_____

_____

_____

_____

7

DESTROYING THE HAUTE COUTURE

The church gradually influenced my identity, but many young people believe they can find their identities in circles that promote vices and violence. To this, we can add the role played by most of the media, which constantly shapes the adolescent psyche, given that youth usually lack the maturity to deal with life's pressures or expectations on their own.

Since my mother was a seamstress, when she taught me how to sew and make clothes, she stressed that all sewing and finishing should be neat. This meant zigzag stitching along the edges so that they didn't fray. She also taught me that in haute couture or high fashion, one could not use a variety of fabrics on the same piece because when they're not the same material, literally one of the two will sooner or later tear or unravel the other.

For example, she emphasized the importance of not mixing wool and silk fabrics or a stiff fabric like canvas or denim with fine linen. She also taught me that every material has its thread direction, and cuts should not be made haphazardly or based on the size of the roll of fabric but according to the thread's direction. Otherwise, the piece would come out crooked, and the work would look unprofessional. Lastly, she taught me that all garment-making has a reason for being haute couture.

But what is happening to fashion now? We find clothing pieces with different fabrics, torn or untucked finishes, different types of buttons, and even faded fabrics. It is becoming more and more commonplace to find pieces with two or more different styles in the same garment. I know that many might see this as something authentic or even avant-garde, but it is instead an example of how original fashions can be destroyed.

I am using this analogy on the destruction of high fashion to emphasize that the world works to destroy God's original design, even if it's at the expense of a garment's quality. But before going on, I want to clear up something: mixing fabrics is not the same as mixing colors.

They are two different ideas. In other words, although high fashion should not mix materials, a garment of the same material can be combined with other colors. Therefore, in no way can we use this allegory about haute couture to justify racism or xenophobia.

This is a very broad topic that I would love to address a little more in-depth in another book to try to expose how these kinds of hatreds, prejudices, and grudges have always damaged the identity of people everywhere. However, what I do wish to highlight now

Regardless of our skin color,
culture, or race, we are all the
same human fabric,
made in the image and
likeness of our Creator.

is that, regardless of our skin color, culture, or race, we are all the same human fabric, made in the image and likeness of our Creator. There are no exceptions to this. We are all loved by Him.

Having clarified this point, let's return to the subject of tailoring. The examples we see on fashion runways today are sustainable trends—styles will remain in place for specific periods. The public always has the final word. A designer can suggest ideas with their outfits, but if the public does not wear them and they do not become popular, these ideas will never stand out.

In the past, we only found style references from relevant people like celebrities who appeared in the media. Nowadays, the Internet, particularly social networks such as Instagram, allows ordinary people to influence the styles in culture. And just like the rest of the art world, fashion is often inspired by the difficulties and challenges of every historical moment.

Some years ago, there were calls for greater racial diversity in the industry. Now the focus is undoubtedly on the issue of gender. And fashion is a sector responsible for most of the stereotypes concerning our image.

However, high fashion now seeks to create works of art through clothing, even if it is unconventional. I view it as just another way of pushing the boundaries in every sense, where what used to be thought of as elegant, visually pleasing, and crafted under the basic principles of pattern making, design, and tailoring is now considered old-fashioned and out of touch. It's a highly competitive industry, and many brands have even lost their line of elegance that they kept throughout the years to fit in with the new trends.

GOD'S PERFECT CONFIGURATION

Our life works in the same way. Everything has an order in the ideal configuration, which was designed perfectly for us by God.

That is why I would like you to reflect for a moment to consider whether it is really worth destroying our original composition to follow a passing fashion. Should we let ourselves be influenced by the media and social networks because we want to look cool? At the end of the day, all fashions also fade.

I'm talking about something much more complex than choosing between a low-cut blouse and a high-necked dress or between a loose-fitting skirt and a tight-fitting pair of pants.

When we talk about changing God's original configuration for us, we are talking about everything that makes us act in ways that go against our nature. Beyond that, adopting these ideas as part of our way of life and our identity hinders God's plans for us.

As I said before, I do not seek to persuade much less criticize people. This includes some groups and communities that I also respect and appreciate as brothers and sisters. And I ask you to love them for who they are—people created and loved by God—before you criticize them either.

I have always considered behaviors or inclinations that do not adhere to that original and perfect plan created by our heavenly Father as unnatural. For example, until now, I have been unable to understand what drives a woman to have an abortion while knowing that she is carrying a life inside of her, or what makes two people engage in same-sex practices and sentimental relationships.

However, I do not want my point to be misconstrued. It is not my desire to point them out or tell them that they are not right, but to expound why it is impossible for me to fully understand their reasons, since our God-given configuration is already perfect, lacking nothing whatsoever. Indeed, it is nothing short of a true miracle that proves His existence.

QUESTIONS FOR REFLECTION

1. How do you see yourself fashioned in God's perfection?

_____

_____

_____

_____

_____

2. List the qualities with which you think God designed you.

_____

_____

_____

_____

_____

8

HOW AND WHEN DOES THE RIGHT PERSON COME ALONG?

Before meeting the man who is now my husband, I met several young men in high school whom I thought were cute. I want to share my experience and what I learned from three relationships with young men with different personalities.

INITIAL ATTRACTION

I liked the first one so much that I fell in love with him, but I never spoke to him. I would just look at him and say to myself, "He's so handsome." Romantic music would make me sigh and think of him. I would doodle hearts and write his name in my notebooks.

He never knew that I was interested in him, and we never even became friends. Every time I wanted to talk to him, I quickly thought, *But how? He is so handsome and popular that it is not even worth trying. He's never going to give me the time of day because I'm fat and ugly.*

Remember how I talked about the difference between who I am and how I see myself in a previous chapter? Well, that was the misconception I had of myself at the time.

Now, I'm sure that because of this, I missed the opportunity to talk to him, get to know him better, and at least establish a nice friendship. I can't say for sure that he would have become my boyfriend, but considering how nice he was to everyone around him, the only one deprived of his friendship due to self-rejection was me.

I learned a great lesson from this: in life, except for God's matchless love, nothing can be perfect. Everything doesn't happen the way we would like it to. And because of my insecurities and fixation on him solely as a boyfriend, I missed out on what could have been a beautiful friendship.

By the age of fourteen, I started to lose weight, but I still didn't consider myself to be pretty because my teeth were dark from the antibiotics.

A BOYFRIEND AND FAMILY FRIENDSHIP

Later on, I met another young man, and we became friends. I also befriended his brothers and sisters. In fact, his younger sister became my best friend at the time. We all spent a lot of time together playing board games until, one night, we went to a party, where he asked me to be his girlfriend, and I said yes. So he was my first boyfriend.

However, we were both very young and immature, and that relationship only lasted a few months. Although it was short-lived, it was still long enough for me to experience and learn that a heart can also hurt from nostalgia.

I cannot deny that it was great while it lasted, though. His family was fun, charismatic, and kept a very good relationship with my parents. In fact, what hurt me the most was when our families separated. At that time, they left Guatemala because their father had a once-in-a-lifetime job opportunity abroad as a surgeon. There was no way to stop the course of things. Besides, it would have been very selfish of me to try to do so.

That experience shut my heart to the idea of ever having a boyfriend again. Around that time, however, I started playing volleyball and saw Cash, my beloved husband, for the first time at a national youth volleyball championship in Retalhuleu. However, I didn't even know his name, so I wasn't in a relationship with him. The only thing I remember thinking about Cash was, "Wow, that little Asian guy can sure play the game."

After that, I went to California to study at Vanden High School. When I returned to Guatemala, I got my teeth partially fixed and started studying at a bilingual school. It wasn't until that point that I started going to a Christian church.

FAILED ATTEMPT

It was following my return from the United States that I met a young man I liked. He was a sportsman, but my heart was not yet entirely healed from the heartache of being separated from my first boyfriend. I asked God for patience and His help so that I could reciprocate the feelings of this new boy.

Loving someone means also
loving them with your head
and not just your heart.

While he continued to be very attentive and thoughtful, I opened up to him, explaining what I was going through. There came the point when I realized the emotional harm I was causing him by waiting to be his girlfriend, and it made me feel even worse.

At this point, I learned that loving someone means also loving them with your head and not just your heart. Depression and disappointment not only affect us but can also bring about great damage to those around us or those who try to get close to us.

From that moment, I made up my mind that the next time I liked someone, I would approach them first and talk to them by presenting myself honestly and sincerely. I would seek God first and then heal my heart before allowing myself to meet anyone else. At the time, I thought, *I know the right boy will come along with whom I will feel right to engage in a healthy relationship as friends and then as boyfriend and girlfriend.*

Even though I had good friends in church, I decided to serve the Lord first and foremost before entering into a relationship. I wanted to achieve my dreams of studying, working, and doing other things as well.

THE RIGHT ONE

Until one day, without my expecting it or even suspecting it, the right boy appeared on my seventeenth birthday. He appeared only when I had stopped thinking about having a boyfriend—when I had placed God first in my life, healed my heart, forgotten about my previous relationships, and, above all, once I had already decided to be happy with myself.

Only then did I know that he was the one whom God had prepared for me. The person with whom I could enjoy an amicable relationship serving the Lord without fear or prejudice, free of worry, doing things right, and being prudent in planning my future. I can say that this was more of a personal decision and a commitment to myself rather than a couple's decision.

How did the right one come along? After growing in my service to God for some time, in the church I was attending in Guatemala City, I again came across that young *chinito*, the Asian kid who I had previously seen playing volleyball in Retalhuleu. To be honest, he had not changed a bit since then; he looked precisely the same. But I saw him differently this time.

Before this, I recall friends at church using him as a reference point to measure how handsome other young men were. For example, whenever we would argue about how nice some guy was, someone would say something like, "What's he like—is he better looking than Cash?" or "Is he sweeter than Cash?" And I would say, "But who is this 'Cash' guy they are always talking about? I don't know any Cash, but this other guy I am seeing is quite handsome."

Until one day, I once again saw the guy named Cash whose name was on the lips of all my friends. It all happened when we arrived late at one of our church services and couldn't find anywhere to sit together with my friend Dinora. The only seats available were next to him. When he saw that we were looking for a place to sit, he kindly guided us to where he was sitting. It was at that moment that I recognized who he was—that great volleyball player! This time, I was ready to introduce myself and talk to him. I was not going to remain alone, silent, and miss out on the desire to get to know him, so I prompted the initial contact myself.

I just want to highlight something here: if you are a woman who is around the same age I was at the time, don't make the mistake I made of being afraid to talk to people as I did with the first guy I liked.

Many young men and women are afraid to take the initiative and talk to someone they want to meet. They don't feel attractive or exciting enough, and they think they will be turned down right away. Then, they keep viewing the person from a distance, like a platonic love, without ever even approaching them.

Others jump ahead, thinking that a hypothetical romantic relationship with that person won't work, even though they haven't even taken the first step! Still others fall prey to the belief that a relationship between the two is not part of God's will and expect more answers than necessary; they think angels should come down from heaven to tell them if that's the right person or not. And if not, the angels should tell them where they *can* find Mr. or Ms. Right.

I want to clear things up for any young men and women who think like this: life does not work that way. In any type of friendship or dating relationship, the first step will always be to get to know the person—not to go steady, get married, break up, or anything of the sort, but simply to get to know each other. Until you get to know each other, you can never be sure how a relationship would turn out, much less understand if they are the person whom God has in store for you.

These types of behaviors indicate that someone is unsure about their identity as an attractive person who can carry out God's best plans and help other people. As we have seen before, their insecurity does not allow them to see how precious they are. You deserve to meet the person you like free of prejudices or fear of failure. After you meet, God can speak to your heart and reveal whether or not they are the young man or woman for you.

By the time I met Cash, I understood the saying, "You snooze, you lose." So without giving it much thought, I approached him and struck up a conversation. "Don't I know you?" I asked. "You play volleyball, right? I also play volleyball and would like to see you play one day." Not one to lose the moment, he said, "Well, I'm playing later today. Would you like to go?" And of course, I said yes.

That's how it all started. I didn't go into hiding like I did when I was younger, nor did I bemoan my previous failed relationship. I took the first step. Volleyball brought us together, and with God's help, we have achieved the rest. Of course, everything happened in an honest and sincere way, always telling the truth, free of any ulterior motives.

My heart was ready. God had healed it, and I was ready to receive the blessing He had for me. Perhaps it was something I could not yet fathom at the time. In fact, I didn't even think about the remote possibility that this *chinito*, the Asian kid, and I could be a couple, but God did. He already had a plan for me since before I was born. He knew that I was spiritually and emotionally well enough to meet a new guy with whom I could develop a relationship.

Many years later, Cash told me that he had tried to approach me before that day in church, but I had seemed to him to be a little too proud. And he'd just say, "Well, it's her loss." What I do know is that our relationship gradually evolved in a very special way, step by step, with everything in its own time.

It was only when I got to know him better that I realized Cash was the answer to a prayer I had made to God when I was nine years old: "God, if I ever have a boyfriend—which I don't know what that is—he should see me as pretty, and love me and love You one hundred percent!" With this, I can testify that God always listens to us regardless of our age, condition, sins, or emotional needs. His will is to always give His children the very best.

He desires to give you a life partner, and I can assure you that when you see that person, our Father will find ways to show you that they are right for you. It will then be up to both of you to care for and nurture that relationship. I had to go through three attempts before meeting the person the Lord had in store for me, so never give up after the first failure.

QUESTIONS FOR REFLECTION

1. Do you have any doubts that the person you are getting to know is the one God has for you?

    _____

    _____

    _____

    _____

    _____

2. Have you talked to God about it? Are you recognizing His signs? Are you listening to Him even if you don't like the answer?

    _____

    _____

    _____

    _____

    _____

9

YOU DESERVE A HEALTHY AND GENUINE RELATIONSHIP

Many people are afraid to start dating because they imagine that it immediately implies marriage. For example, I told one of my friends, "That young man wants to be your boyfriend," and she panicked because she interpreted this to mean he wanted to tie the knot right away. The reality is that the beauty of dating is found in getting to know another person before taking any important steps.

Every marital relationship begins long before declaring your love for the other person or giving them a ring. It starts with a friendship. It is a process that should not be rushed because only by

Self-confidence and believing in yourself are foundational for any healthy relationship.

experiencing it will you truly know if you both want to be together. Friendships and courtships are about getting to know each other and being transparent about who you are without trying to be someone else.

What do you believe about yourself? How much do you value your gifts and abilities? How much do you value a good education? God keeps helping me to believe in myself, my abilities, my studies, and my family. Self-confidence and believing in yourself are foundational for any healthy relationship. I am certain that these were key ingredients for Cash to notice me at the time. If I had continued with my insecurities from childhood and puberty, I am pretty sure that even today at my age, I would still be single, no matter how much I exercised or watched my diet.

At this point, I would like to take a moment and ask you the following questions:

+ Do you really believe in yourself and your abilities?

+ Can you be a self-sufficient woman and be attractive in the eyes of God and other people?

+ What do you have to offer in a relationship?

+ What treasures lie within you just waiting to be discovered by a special person?

+ What is it about you that causes other people to say, "I just love that about her"?

Whether you are a woman or a man, every one of us has a certain unique factor that is pleasing to others and makes them want to get to know us. For example, you might not be too tall, but if you have a charming smile, you will have the upper hand.

No one wants to live with
a complicated person, no
matter how pretty she is.

On the other hand, even if you're a fashion model, if you have an arrogant and insufferable character, you won't even get a second date with a person you like.

Although everyone has certain qualities, you should take care not to draw excessive attention to yourself. Learn to be someone who respects herself and others. By following this rule, you can be sure that others will admire you in the way you deserve to be admired. If you are too eager to show off your assets—whether it's intelligence, charisma, or physical attributes—or if you are rebellious, disrespectful, and always contentious without any critical reason for it, provoking fights and demanding attention, you're likely to get negative results.

I assure you that no one wants to live with a complicated person, no matter how pretty she is. You don't need to be perfect, but do your best to be polite, pleasant, and genuine.

I'll give you a couple of specific examples. Suppose you are a distrustful, controlling woman who always believes that your boyfriend is being unfaithful. This can easily rob you of your peace and ultimately damage your relationship. Likewise, if you are a woman who is resentful about anything—for example, if your boyfriend fails to notice your new haircut or a personal achievement—consider times when you might have done the same thing. Perhaps you have forgotten or overlooked something important to him on another occasion, whether it was his birthday, a package in the mail, or his mother's name.

FINDING LOVE

First Timothy 4:12 says, "*Let no one despise your youth, but be an example to the believers in word, in conduct, in love, in spirit, in faith, in purity.*" Youth is a stage in life that we are meant to enjoy, but it can also be a time of confusion and misinformation without good marriage role models who we can respect and admire.

Thank God for making you different, and don't forget that feeling attraction for someone is normal, so never feel bad about it.

How do you know if the person you are attracted to is right for you? How do you know if your relationship is healthy and whole? Ask yourself the following questions:

+ Are you proud of that person? No lasting relationship can be based on shame. You may like someone, but if you don't feel really comfortable in public with that person, they are not the one for you. The person you want as your life partner needs to be someone you admire because once you're married, you won't be able to hide them. On the other hand, you too must take care of yourself physically, emotionally, and spiritually so that you are likable to other people.

+ Do you respect that person? When you really love someone, you are not selfish or abusive. You always think of how to please the other person and treat them well, with respect and purity. If you do not respect them, what you are feeling is only temporary passion.

+ Do you fully trust their love and faithfulness? When I was Cash's girlfriend, there were some young women who threatened to *steal him away* from me. However, the confidence he inspired in me made me feel good about myself. If I had been jealous during our relationship, I would have suffered even more once we were married. If you are feeling jealous when your man talks to another woman, for example, you may be insecure or have a wrong perception of yourself. If you feel that your jealousy is justified, I encourage you to seek the advice of a spiritual leader. But the first step is to have complete confidence in who you are and what you have to offer.

If you are dirty, unkempt, or have no life aspirations, work to overcome these issues.

+ Do you have affinity with each other? Can you talk for hours and never run out of topics? Does time seem too short when you are together? The Bible teaches us that it is important not to be unequally yoked. (See 2 Corinthians 6:14.) Two people should share a vision of life and complement each other. Perhaps you have the patience that the other person lacks, and he offers you the steadiness that you do not have. Love is not automatic. It is expressed with deeds and words. It must be cultivated by sharing time together.

+ Do you always seek their well-being? Remember that love involves generous giving. If you act selfishly or in a self-centered way, it means that you do not really love the person. When starting a relationship, never think about what you can receive but what you can offer and learn to be pleasant so that the person seeks your company. To give and receive expressions of love without regret, join someone with whom you share the vision and effort to achieve something great.

+ Do your parents approve? When I wonder how my mom allowed me to get married at age nineteen, I think she must have seen some signs of maturity in me and Cash—from our respectful treatment of each other to our discipline and commitment. However, the decision to marry isn't always an easy one. Wisdom is found in an abundance of advice. Other people's perspectives can be very valuable, and even better if it comes from those who love you the most. Your parents' advice may be the best you get.

+ Are you willing to wait until the time is right? When a person is in a hurry to get married, it may be because things are not going too well. The rush may be sexual or simply to

No one and nothing can
ever define you. Only an
infinite catalyst can give true
meaning to your life.

escape a troubled family situation. True love knows how to wait for the right moment. God gives us the best example of this by sending His Son at the right time.

+ Do you feel at ease when you think about getting married? Draw near to the Lord to help you visualize your married life with the person you have chosen. The image that comes to mind should be one that fills you with peace. The Bible says that we can boldly come before His throne of grace and ask Him for our mate, so do this free of fear.

+ Do you feel the same way about each other? Make sure that what you feel is reciprocated. If you have any doubts about this, you can ask the person directly about their intentions and if they feel the same way you do. But if you are both looking for different ways of relating to one another, the best thing would be to separate or otherwise maintain a pleasant and genuine friendship.

Meditate on and answer these questions. They will help you reflect and have a more objective view of your specific situation with your partner. Remember that if God is at the center of your relationship, you are bound to be happy.

A PERSONAL DECISION

Entering into a relationship is a personal decision. Although some people can offer you advice, no one should make that decision for you. Focus on who you are in your identity and visualize how your identity will be complemented by the other person's identity. Don't forget that no one and nothing can ever define you. Only an *infinite catalyst* can give true meaning to your life.

Reflecting on these things will help you make better decisions. If you like to play a sport, practice it. If you want to meet the Lord, go to church. If you want to meet someone, talk to them. But make sure your first decision is always to seek God. I can guarantee what the Bible says: everything else will follow if you *"seek first the kingdom of God and His righteousness"* (Matthew 6:33).

10

A WOMAN WITH WHOM YOU WANT TO LIVE

When I first started going steady with the man who is now my husband, a young woman approached me to tell me that she really liked him and would do everything in her power to "take him away" from me. My response was swift: "If you are so set and determined, don't think twice and go ahead." For my part, I was pretty sure of myself, and that confidence was what strengthened my relationship with Cash. However, it wasn't long before we faced a much more complicated test that matured us before we even made the decision to commit to marriage.

My commitment to God was genuine, so even though Cash and I broke up, I never stopped going to church.

A year into our relationship, Cash told me that he was going to pray to confirm whether it was God's will for us to remain together. It is a valid request because marriage is such a serious commitment, but I was direct in my answer; I told him that if he did not want be with me, he should just tell me. He said something along the lines of, "Let's pray to see if it's God's will," but I told him no. "That's all baloney," I said. "If you don't want anything to do with me, then let's break up." And we did; we broke up.

I was challenged by the fact that he needed to get an answer from God to continue our relationship. All I could see at the time were his doubts about me. Cash was always a great leader in the church we attended, so he was faced with the dilemma of whether I was a woman who would live up to his plans to serve the Lord.

Although I was always very dedicated and devoted to God, back then I was not known as a great leader. And while Cash stood out among all of the other leaders, I was rather shy and hardly noticed in comparison to other young women in the church, many of whom had worship, preaching, or leadership skills that were remarkable. To be honest, however, I often suspected that some of them were trying to get Cash's attention.

I can't deny that I also tried to show Cash my commitment to the ministry, but in light of his doubts, I wasn't going to persuade him, much less beg him not to break up with me.

My commitment to God was genuine, so even though Cash and I broke up, I never stopped going to church or meeting with my friends, including him. My life continued pretty much the same as it had been. In fact, when we broke up, I was able to recognize how timely and necessary our separation was because it helped us value our friendship even more.

During our time apart, I prayed for Cash to find a woman who would love him, and I prayed that God would show him the path

Wanting to live with a person
does not necessarily mean
you can live with them.

he should follow. I never stopped going to the youth group, nor did I stop serving God in the children's ministry. I loved the Lord with all my heart, although I must confess that I was still in love with Cash too. So one day, I prayed to the Lord that if Cash was the man with whom I could live, marry, and serve in the church, that He would keep him for me; otherwise, that He would take him out of my heart. I also prayed for the year not to end without getting an answer from God.

Psalm 37:4 says, *"Delight yourself also in the LORD, and He shall give you the desires of your heart."* Back then, I still could not grasp the magnitude of the benefit of delighting in God and having Him respond to me almost immediately because that's exactly what happened. God kept Cash for me, and we started dating once again before the year was over.

God answered me in the most direct way possible. One day, after a month of being separated, Cash asked me if he could walk me home after the youth service, to which I agreed. That same night, he declared his love for me again, and we began an even stronger relationship. From that day on, he visited me in the evenings and accompanied me in my study time. Together, we strengthened our desire to serve God and the people in the church.

BEING ABLE TO LIVE WITH SOMEONE VS. WANTING TO LIVE WITH SOMEONE

Cash told me that during this process, God showed him the difference between a person you *want* to live with and a person you *can* live with. Wanting to live with someone does not necessarily mean you can live with them. He was often advised: "Think of a woman who can help you in your leadership and ministry," but he thought, "I just want a woman to love, to marry, and have a family with."

Given his spiritual development and his desire to evangelize, he also wondered many times if what he really wanted in life was to marry and engage in a formal relationship. From a very young age, Cash dreamed of becoming an evangelist and perhaps thought that having a relationship would stand in the way of his plans.

However, that evening as he walked me home after the youth meeting, we reaffirmed our individual dreams—mine was to study and work, while his was to preach the Word of the Lord. We were able to happily commit ourselves to one another with greater confidence.

Our courtship, including the time we were apart, lasted two years and four months. It began when I was seventeen and he was twenty-one. He was always welcome in my home, and I always respected his desire to preach the Word of God. I was fascinated by his desire to serve and his self-confidence as a person.

Deciding to wed was not difficult because we were both responsible and disciplined, despite our youth, and we believed in the rewards that come from hard work and effort. It's also worth mentioning that our families supported us every step of the way. Without fully realizing the responsibility that a commitment of such magnitude would entail, we married when I was nineteen on January 25, 1986, in a ceremony held in the church we were attending, with five hundred people in attendance. There was no wedding reception; instead, we served cake to our guests, who included our friends, family, and church leaders. Later, at my mother's house, we ate and celebrated with our families as we prepared for our honeymoon in Guatemala's interior.

Our first wedding gift was our wedding bands, given to us by a lady who owned a jewelry store. The cakes we shared with all our guests were also gifts. Another wedding gift we received was a week's stay in a chalet by the shores of Lake Atitlan for our honeymoon. Other gifts helped us furnish our house during our first years of marriage. For example, my older sister gave us her refrigerator. To this day, I am extremely grateful to God and every person who bestowed their love on us through those presents.

QUESTIONS FOR REFLECTION

1. Do you know the family of the person you are considering for marriage? What do you know about where they come from?

   _____

   _____

   _____

   _____

   _____

2. How much do you know about their customs, ideas, and important matters such as work and home life?

   _____

   _____

   _____

   _____

3. Is this a person you want to live with or can live with?

   _____

   _____

   _____

   _____

11

IMPERFECT BUT RIGHT MARRIAGES

Anewlywed couple's first task is to adapt to one another—as different and independent people—to form a single unit without sacrificing each one's individuality.

There is no better way to learn the course of marriage than in the school of life, gleaning from marriages all around us. I got my first example from my parents' marriage. Perhaps there are other sources we think we can learn from, such as soap operas, TV series, plays, or books, but there's nothing that can top seeing a marriage first-hand, lived out by our parents or guardians.

A newlywed couple's first
task is to adapt to one
another to form a single unit
without sacrificing each
one's individuality.

A marriage is made up of two completely different people, with two different backgrounds, customs, and origins but with every right to come together and get to know each other. The Scriptures do not give us instructions on how to engage in courtship, but they do speak of commitment, respect, and affection between a man and a woman in marriage with the same purpose for God.

Marriages in my family were very normal, each with their differences, victories, setbacks, affinities, and difficulties. I grew up watching the completely dysfunctional marital relationships between my parents and my uncle and his wife. Perhaps that is why I drew my own conclusions on the subject at a very young age and decided not to believe in marriage. However, what marriage is ever really perfect? There is a phrase my husband often uses that reminds me of this: "There are no perfect marriages, just right ones."

TWO BARBIES AND A KEN

We should not obsess over the ghosts of our parents' failed or dysfunctional relationship. Just because they had issues does not mean that we will repeat the process. Our relationships may be better or even worse than theirs, but we are not destined to repeat the same patterns.

Many years ago, I met some friends on a long road trip. It took several hours to drive to our destination, so we had enough time to talk about everything, laugh out loud, and even be genuine with each other and cry.

Julia, one of my friends, began to tell us something very curious about her childhood. Her father was a married man who had an extramarital affair with a woman who was much younger; she was eighteen and he was thirty-eight when they met. Despite the age difference, she fell in love with him, and they had four children together. Their third child was Julia.

From a very young age, Julia wondered why her father never lived with them, why they never saw him for more than two days in a row, and why he always left that same night if he came to visit them one day. Then one day, while she was still very young, Julia became aware of the truth although she didn't fully understand it yet: her dad, besides having an absorbing job, also had another wife and family. However, in her childhood innocence, she did not know that she, her mother, and her siblings were the *other family*, not the primary or first family.

Nonetheless, Julia came to see this as such a typical situation that when her father came to visit them one day, she asked him for a Barbie doll for her Ken. On his next visit, her dad brought her the new doll while noticing that Julia already had a Barbie. "Why did you ask me for a Barbie for your Ken if you already had one?" he asked, to which Julia replied that she couldn't play in the right way with them because she was still missing Ken's other wife.

Now, with two Barbies and a Ken, the set was complete. Sometimes, Ken would get into bed with a Barbie on either side of him. At other times, the Barbies would be in different beds, and Julia vividly remembers having her Ken doll tell the blonde Barbie, "I love you, sweetheart, but I've got to go. Don't wake the children up; just kiss them for me." And then he would jump into the brunette Barbie's bed and tell her, "I'm here, my love."

As time went by and Julia grew older, she finally understood who the *other family* really was, which impacted her identity for a long time. Julia never formalized her dating relationships and constantly avoided commitment because she didn't want to be one of the *other* women. As a teenager, she grew up believing that all men were the same, and she was not willing to become a single mom like her mother and her mother's two sisters.

One day, during her teenage years, Julia accepted Jesus into her heart and immediately felt His embrace as a father embraces his children. It was then that she asked the Lord to give her the opportunity to form a traditional family.

God answered her with a solid marriage of thirty-two years, and she is very proud of the two children she and her husband have raised. In addition, Julia and her husband serve the Lord and many families in their church. Julia's testimony shows us that there are no patterns or failed models that can ever define us once God is in our lives.

GOD IS MADE PERFECT IN OUR WEAKNESS

Unlike Julia, I never thought that all men were the same, but I did shy away from the commitment of marriage and all it implied. At the time, I would have settled with just having a boyfriend and developing the professional areas of my life. And if I used to think that way when I was young, I can imagine how young women must think about marriage today.

Since I did not used to believe in marriage, the Lord was made perfect in my weakness because I am now a pastor who encourages marriage wherever I go. I know it sounds ironic, but this is also how God operates sometimes. His Word says:

And He said to me, "My grace is sufficient for you, for My strength is made perfect in weakness." Therefore most gladly I will rather boast in my infirmities, that the power of Christ may rest upon me. (2 Corinthians 12:9)

In January 2021, my husband and I celebrated our thirty-fifth wedding anniversary. We have reached this milestone thanks to God's grace and love as well as the love that we willingly express to each other every day, in our words and deeds, never holding back. We realized that more than just being two individuals married for many years, we are life partners who have learned to accept and tolerate each other's differences, thus achieving an atmosphere of respect and harmony.

God dealt with me in three areas that have so far helped me maintain a healthy marriage according to His will.

1. REJECT DEFIANCE AND FOOLISHNESS

A rebellious person does not accept advice and readily expresses their disagreement. They tend to repeat conflictive behaviors and become aggressive at times. They defy even their own parents and disobey established rules. We are all born with this rebellious nature. Proverbs 22:15 says, *"Foolishness is bound up in the heart of a child; the rod of correction will drive it far from him."*

Foolishness is synonymous with recklessness and disobedience, but it is also a sign of low intelligence, the opposite of the wisdom that God gives us. Correction, on the other hand, brings understanding. If we do not accept the Lord's correction, nor that of our parents, life itself will end up correcting us.

I urge you to accept God's correction without any resentment toward Him. It is the same as any parent's correction of a child, just as Scripture tells us:

> *For whom the LORD loves He corrects, just as a father the son in whom he delights.* (Proverbs 3:12)

Remember that wisdom first comes as a result of the fear of the Lord. Proverbs 31:30 says, *"Charm is deceitful and beauty is passing, but a woman who fears the LORD, she shall be praised."*

If any of you lacks wisdom, let him ask of God, who gives to all liberally and without reproach, and it will be given to him. But let him ask in faith, with no doubting.   (James 1:5–6)

2. GIVING GOD A PROMINENT PLACE

King Solomon wrote:

Two are better than one, because they have a good reward for their labor. For if they fall, one will lift up his companion. But woe to him who is alone when he falls, for he has no one to help him up. Again, if two lie down together, they will keep warm; but how can one be warm alone? Though one may be overpowered by another, two can withstand him. And a threefold cord is not quickly broken.   (Ecclesiastes 4:9–12)

When I first noticed this Bible passage, my heart began to believe in God's covenant with man and woman in marriage and the benefits that come together with it. It made me see the importance of marriage in anyone's life, as it is not only our will as individuals, but also the Lord's will—so much so that He instituted it.

When I saw Cash for the second time in church, I felt attracted to him. And by then, I felt confident in myself, prompting me to get to know him better. He liked me too...and so far, so good. In fact, if we had wanted to, we could have remained together for the rest of our lives, had children, and formed a family as we do now, and apparently nothing would have been different, although

I can't really be sure of that either. For example, if we had not had the benefit of the commitment that only marriage can provide, we might not have survived even two years before realizing how complicated it is to live with another person.

However, the biggest single difference between being married and being single lies in our covenant with God. As a woman, if I were to live in a relationship outside of marriage, I would be greatly limiting the blessing of making Him a part of our life together. That is why, right from the start, God established a covenant between man and woman. We see it from the time of Adam and Eve.

It has always been God's will that every man and woman leave their parents to enter into a covenant of marriage, as Jesus told the Pharisees who were testing Him:

> And He answered and said to them, "Have you not read that He who made them at the beginning 'made them male and female,' and said, 'For this reason a man shall leave his father and mother and be joined to his wife, and the two shall become one flesh'? So then, they are no longer two but one flesh. Therefore what God has joined together, let not man separate."   (Matthew 19:4–6)

3. THE FRUIT OF SUBMISSION

The Lord teaches us that a person in submission recognizes a designated authority and understands that everything created by God has an order. When I first learned that a husband is the head of a marriage, I immediately knew that God was calling me to fulfill His command despite being an independent, self-sufficient woman with a strong character. In my parents' relationship, I saw greater authority in my mother than in my father, but the Lord delegated the headship of marriage to the man. In his letter to the Ephesians, Paul compares the relationship between husband and wife to our relationship to Jesus as our role model and head of the church.

> *Wives, submit to your own husbands, as to the Lord. For the husband is head of the wife, as also Christ is head of the church; and He is the Savior of the body. Therefore, just as the church is subject to Christ, so let the wives be to their own husbands in everything. Husbands, love your wives, just as Christ also loved the church and gave Himself for her.*
>
> (Ephesians 5:22–25)

Submission implies creating a new bond in which each element becomes complementary to the other. It is also worth highlighting that submission is not domination, subjugation, contempt, or subordination. In other words, by being subject to her husband, a woman should not accept mistreatment from him in the form of any physical, psychological, or emotional abuse, nor should she subject her husband to such abuse. Many confuse submission with subordination, which is erroneous, since the husband is as subject to his wife as she is to him. (See Ephesians 5:21.) Submission is the fruit of both parties and their conjugal rights. (See 1 Corinthians 7:2–4.)

In Colossians 3:18, the Bible urges wives to submit to their husbands *"as is fitting in the Lord."* Peter's first epistle explains the reason for this:

> *Wives, likewise, be submissive to your own husbands, that even if some do not obey the word, they, without a word, may*

Submission implies creating
a new unit in which
each element becomes
complementary to the other.

be won by the conduct of their wives, when they observe your chaste conduct accompanied by fear. Do not let your adornment be merely outward—arranging the hair, wearing gold, or putting on fine apparel—rather let it be the hidden person of the heart, with the incorruptible beauty of a gentle and quiet spirit, which is very precious in the sight of God. For in this manner, in former times, the holy women who trusted in God also adorned themselves, being submissive to their own husbands, as Sarah obeyed Abraham, calling him lord, whose daughters you are if you do good and are not afraid with any terror. (1 Peter 3:1–6)

As I mentioned earlier, recognizing our role within the marriage covenant brings with it significant benefits. God says to a woman without children or abandoned by her husband, *"Your Maker is your husband"* (Isaiah 54:5). God takes the husband's place should he ever leave or reject her, but He never takes the place of a wife for the man. The Lord has put women in a privileged position so that we can be honored by our husbands. That is why we should submit to them, freely and without fear, for submission is a blessing and not an imposition.

As with the husband, every woman should bear the fruit of submission to someone in a position of authority, such as a father, a teacher, a boss, a policeman, a religious leader, or a president, to mention a few. In one way or another, these authorities are appointed by God to establish order.

WHAT IF MARRIAGE ISN'T FOR ME?

If you still don't believe in marriage and are convinced that it is definitely not for you, I respect your decision, and those who love you should respect it too. In these pages, I have sought to share what marriage has been like for me and how my identity has been gradually transformed throughout different stages of my life, including almost thirty-six years of marriage.

But if marriage and raising a family are definitely not your thing, never trick yourself into believing that it is the only way to keep a covenant with God. There is always the possibility of serving Him and blessing others in another way, as 1 Corinthians 7:34 says:

> *There is a difference between a wife and a virgin. The unmarried woman cares about the things of the Lord, that she may be holy both in body and in spirit. But she who is married cares about the things of the world—how she may please her husband.*

QUESTIONS FOR REFLECTION

1. What personal characteristics have you had to work on to achieve harmony in your marriage?

_____

_____

_____

_____

_____

2. Do you believe that marriage has brought about changes in your identity?

_____

_____

_____

_____

12

A LIFELONG COVENANT

Right from the start, my husband and I came up with a family budget. He had just launched a computer company when this type of technological knowledge was not yet widespread and mainstream in Guatemala. So it was not easy for us to manage household expenses. After working through some figures, we concluded that I should also work outside the home to help meet our budget.

I did not take it badly—quite the opposite. I loved it since I have always enjoyed working. In fact, in my parents' home, I was raised to be a responsible, hardworking woman. I knew that as dedicated as I was to my marriage, I was not ready to stay at home all day with just housework to occupy my time.

I always had a mindset of producing and making the most of my time. So shortly after returning from our honeymoon, I got a job with a cotton gin company and then later worked for a nylon Oxford cloth importer. I worked until I became pregnant with our first child, one year after we were married. My plan was to continue working until my belly started to show, but the discomforts of pregnancy prevented me from doing so.

One thing I do remember about that first year of marriage is that I earned a little more money than Cash did, and thanks to that, we were both able to cover our expenses.

But this was not the only way God provided for us. At the time, we were living in a neighborhood known as Santa Monica, in a one-level house located in Zone 11 of Guatemala City. It was a comfortably priced home; while other people were paying an average of Q1200 (about $154) for rent in that same sector, we only paid Q700 (about $90) for a house the same size as our neighbors'.[1] Back then, Q500 was an enormous difference and, of course, a significant saving that would have been a relief for any family in better conditions than ours. God alone knows why our rent was lower than everyone else's!

Nonetheless, there were always other expenses to cover. Something I remember quite well in those early years was the challenge of commuting to get our errands covered. Since we only had one car that my husband used for work, I had to wait until Friday to go grocery shopping. When January 1987 came along and I became pregnant with our first son, Carlos Enrique "Cashito," the need to improve our financial situation became even more evident.

---

1. At today's exchange rate, one Guatemalan quetzal is equivalent to about 13 cents in U.S. currency.

No paycheck could ever
compare to the greatest
benefit of a decision like this:
I had the pleasure of raising
my son.

QUITTING WORK: A DIFFICULT DECISION

God once again was faithful to bless our marriage covenant with a very simple lesson. In addition to the discomforts of my pregnancy, the decision to stop working and devote myself completely to my pregnancy and home was based on logical reasoning: when we drew up a new budget, we realized that if I were to continue working, it would be more expensive to cover the costs of a day care center, a maid, transportation for both of us to get around, and a myriad of other expenses, greatly exceeding our budget.

Since I still had a strong desire to work and was raised as a very proactive woman, I must say that it was not an easy decision. In fact, it later brought on an identity crisis. But I thank God for granting me the understanding—and my husband for insisting on it throughout the pregnancy—that lovingly and patiently raising our son was the best decision in the long run.

No matter how large it is, no paycheck could ever compare to the greatest benefit of a decision like this: I had the pleasure of bringing up my son in a loving home where he always had me to care for all of his needs. And as if that were not enough, God's hand did not stop blessing us supernaturally, as I was able to witness with my husband. He engaged in new fruitful business ideas, providing us with much stability and economic security. Gradually, as the years went by, the computer company was followed by the sale of life insurance policies and later by our own men's clothing company.

It is also worth noting that although I was a woman devoted to my home, I also took on an active role in each of these business endeavors during my "free time," performing a wide variety of tasks that ranged from organizing files and reviewing Cash's schedule to interviewing his potential employees.

But God's blessing—which I attribute to being under the marriage covenant—also blessed us with health. I remember one Christmas in those early years when my son got food poisoning after eating some bad grapes, and we had to take him to the hospital. Although we thought it was going to be something serious, praise God, he swiftly recovered.

GOD AT THE TOP OF THE LIST

Both my husband and I are confident and testify that each of these blessings was the result of putting God first in our budget with our tithes and offerings. Literally for every budget we made, God was always at the top of the list. We can testify that our Father is a faithful God, a covenant God who always keeps His promises eventually. Our faith and our first fruits on the altar caused the gates of heaven to open and bless us when we needed it the most. As Proverbs 3:9–10 tells us, *"Honor the LORD with your possessions, and with the firstfruits of all your increase; so your barns will be filled with plenty, and your vats will overflow with new wine."*

RENEWED LOVE

As of this writing, Cash and I are nearing our thirty-sixth wedding anniversary and the end of our fourth stage of marital love, according to Dr. Frank Minirth and the other psychiatrists who wrote *Passages of Marriage.*[2]

They classified marital love into five stages: 1. "young love" for the first two years of marriage; 2. "realistic love" for three to ten years; 3. "comfortable love" for eleven to twenty-five years; 4. "renewed love" for twenty-six to thirty-five years; and 5. "transcendent love" for a marriage lasting thirty-six years or more.

2. Dr. Frank Minirth et al., *Passages of Marriage: Five Growth Stages That Will Take Your Marriage to Greater Intimacy and Fulfillment* (Nashville, TN: Thomas Nelson Inc., 1991).

Each stage comes with its own challenges. Newlyweds must overcome as many difficulties as a couple who have been married over fifty years.

Cash and I are culminating the stage of our "renewed love" and will soon enter the stage of "transcendent love."

PHYSICAL CHANGES IN MARRIAGE

By the time I married, I had long since overcome my hang-ups about my physical appearance. I was already accustomed to the discipline of playing sports and eating right as much as possible. However, the first traumas during marriage are often the result of the physical effects of pregnancy and childbirth. In my case, although I had two standard deliveries, I also had a C-section that left me with a very deep scar. All of this could have significantly affected my mindset and my body's appearance. Still, I took care of myself as much as possible with therapy, exercise, and a healthy diet.

When I turned forty-two, I learned that I was both nearsighted and had blurry or distorted vision. Right up until that moment, I had always been known for my excellent eyesight. For the first time, I realized that I was no longer a young girl and would soon begin to experience other issues that come with aging.

Sometime later, I suffered digestion problems because my body had stopped processing some foods well, which had never been an issue in the past. Later, I had skin problems and became allergic to almost anything. I could go on and on with other issues, but I hope there won't be any more!

We all seem to reach this time of ailments after age forty. It is then that we see the true importance of leading a fit, wholesome life beyond trying to maintain a magazine-worthy figure. Above all, we should be consistent about our need for a healthy diet, the

We should be consistent
about our need for a healthy
diet, the right amount of
sleep, and regular exercise.

right amount of sleep, and regular exercise. We must continually work on ourselves and not neglect our need for self-care.

LEARNING TO DEAL WITH STRESS

During these fast-paced times, it is not uncommon to see teenage couples who are stressed out, even falling into symptoms of depression. Today, more than ever, it is common to see young people who, by the age of twelve or thirteen, trigger a shooting at school or in a public place, take the lives of several people, and then decide to commit suicide.

Some young married couples decide that they cannot bear the emotional burden of being united to one person for life, so they get divorced within a year.

For older couples, the consequences of stressful situations go beyond physical changes. Financial turmoil, the loss of a child, and other situations can cause a lot of pressure in a marriage that the couple must learn to manage. It is not easy to identify stress triggers. Still, we can generally attribute them to a lack of intimacy, job loss, illness, legal problems, and seemingly harmless changes such as retiring or moving to a new house or a different city.

We must first learn to live with the crises that occur during different stages of marriage. We might not always have a lifetime to repair a situation, so learning to deal with it and recognizing the times to give in should be a priority for married couples.

My marriage to Cash has had its share of conflicts, differences, and crises. Just like every other marriage, it has not been perfect... but that is a subject for another book.

QUESTIONS FOR REFLECTION

1. Do you think marriage should be "perfect," or do you have realistic expectations?

   _____

   _____

   _____

   _____

   _____

2. Which situations discussed in this chapter have you had to face in your own marriage? How have you overcome them?

   _____

   _____

   _____

   _____

13

THE MIRACLE OF BEING A MOTHER

From the moment of conception, maternity becomes the most significant factor for preserving our species. Of course, it dramatically influences the identity of every woman who experiences it. It can cause various physical and psychological changes throughout her body, such as a swollen belly, stretch marks, mood swings, cravings or dislikes for certain smells and foods, and so on.

This characteristic of giving birth with pain began when Adam and Eve disobeyed God in the garden of Eden.

To the woman He said: "I will greatly multiply your sorrow and your conception; in pain you shall bring forth children; your desire shall be for your husband, and he shall rule over you."   (Genesis 3:16)

THE IMPORTANCE OF PLANNING

I once heard a young girl, who was no more than thirteen or fourteen years old, say something that gave me chills. "When I grow up," she said, "I'm only going to have two children, a boy and a girl. One with Rubén and the other with Pedro." (I've changed their names to protect their identities.) That's literally what she said as she pointed her finger at them. Although this happened twenty years ago, I still remember how shocked I was by her statement.

Years later, that naïve young girl grew up and kept true to her word, although halfheartedly. She did have a boy and a girl, one of them with Rubén and the other with a certain Arthur who was not in her plans and never saw her again.

Curiously, that girl was able to hit one of her targets. But real life is not as simple as choosing whether to have a child with this person or that person and thinking everything will be fine. Life is much harder if we are reckless with our sexuality, don't maintain a healthy relationship with a partner, and don't engage in responsible family planning.

Women need to address the issue of healthy family planning. I have known several clinical methods, one of which damaged my kidneys. Therefore, if you decide to plan your family, it's crucial to talk to your doctor and pay attention to the warning signs of side effects and your body's reactions to whatever method you use. I have seen very good results with the Billings ovulation method,

The decision to have
a child is not something to be
taken lightly.

also called the *natural method*, which usually works for a woman with regular ovulation cycles.

The decision to have a child is not something to be taken lightly. Before getting married, couples who wish to have children should decide when to do so and then consult with a professional to determine the best family planning method to use based on their individual physiology.

In addition, couples should be prudent and realistic about the enormous commitment that comes with parenthood and make decisions consistent with their situation. Although a woman may dream about becoming a mother, she should think twice before getting pregnant if, for example, her doctor warns her that the baby could develop a deformity within the womb. In addition to medical considerations, there are also social and economic ones to keep in mind. For instance, if a couple is short on resources and has a tight budget, they may want to wait before having children.

In short, there are many factors that can have a considerable impact on our identity, as well as that of our offspring, when procreating without engaging in family planning.

Some may say, "I'm pregnant! No problem—God will provide." Yes, it's true that *"with God all things are possible"* (Matthew 19:26); He loves all His children and will provide them with all sustenance. (See Philippians 4:19.) However, this does not mean that we should throw all reasoning out the window and not act according to His wisdom.

That is why, when it comes to having children, we should act with the intelligence that the Lord expects of us in any life situation. Now, I am not trying to discourage anyone from having children if they have the desire and means to form a family, but there are different ways and times to do so.

Is it a smart decision to remain childless? I know people who think that the only disadvantage to not having children is that there will always be some family member who is constantly pestering you, asking, "When am I going to get a grandchild?" or "When will you give me a little nephew?"

Professor David Barash, an expert in psychology and evolutionary biology at the University of Washington and author of the book *The Whisperings Within*, was asked why more people are choosing not to have children. He said, "It's not surprising in any way because it demonstrates the most remarkable characteristic of the human species: the ability to say no…Throughout history, human beings have not had the luxury of deciding whether or not to reproduce; simply engaging in a sexual relationship was enough to do so. However, movements have arisen that try to demonstrate that the desire to be a mother, or what we usually call maternal instinct, is a cultural rather than a biological inclination."

However, Psalm 127:3 says, *"Behold, children are a heritage from the LORD, the fruit of the womb is a reward."*

Children are a miracle. The complexity of conception is astonishing. One milliliter of semen contains between 15 and 200 million sperm cells. During sexual intercourse, only one sperm cell will fertilize a woman's ovum. If this is not a miracle, then I don't know what is. Something so precise and perfect can only be God's handiwork. Scripture tells us:

> *My frame was not hidden from You, when I was made in secret, and skillfully wrought in the lowest parts of the earth. Your eyes saw my substance, being yet unformed. And in Your book they all were written, the days fashioned for me, when as yet there were none of them.*   (Psalm 139:15–16)

Being a mother is not a
spiritual matter, much less a
religious one,
but being a mother is a purely
natural matter.

I CAN'T HAVE ANY CHILDREN

In the Old Testament, the first book of Samuel contains the story of a married woman named Hannah who was unable to have children. Such a situation can be frustrating for any woman, directly affecting her identity as an instrument sent by God to give life. For a woman who longs to be a mother, childlessness can become the infinite catalyst for an unhappy life.

That was the case for Hannah until the prophet Eli told her that the God of Israel would grant her request to bear a son. And she believed his word. (See 1 Samuel 1:17–20.) At this point, her faith was a decisive ingredient for the miracle to take place. That is how the prophet Samuel was born.

Now, there are more medical and scientific resources in our day and age than Hannah had in her time that can offer hope for couples struggling with infertility. Even so, the miracle only comes from the Lord.

At Casa de Dios, we hold a retreat specifically to minister to and help couples who are unable to have children for one reason or another. And I have witnessed firsthand how the Lord has worked miraculously in people who have been trying to conceive for many years.

I'M A SINGLE MOM

A mother is a mother regardless of her situation. Her work begins even before childbirth. It's a mother's job to care for, nurture, and instruct her children while loving them unconditionally.

A mother has these innate qualities to love and nurture her children, regardless of the color of her hair or skin tone, whether she is wealthy or poor, single, married, or divorced, or if she is a professional, or even believes that she's a child of God or not. Being a mother is not a spiritual matter, much less a religious one, but being a mother is a purely natural matter.

Even so, God's presence is vital, particularly for single mothers. In 2012, the *Journal of Marriage and the Family* published a study drawn from a sample of 1,134 single mothers and concluded that mothers who attend religious services engaged "in parenting practices that promote positive child development." It said:

> Religious participation was associated with greater involvement with children, reduced parenting stress, and a lower likelihood of engaging in corporal punishment. Young children raised by mothers who frequently attended religious services were less likely to display problem behaviors, and this relationship was partially mediated by increased child involvement, lower stress, and less frequent corporal punishment.[3]

Likewise, a report published that same year by Child Trends shows that regardless of financial status, single mothers who received continual emotional support raised successful children who tended to exhibit high social competence and academic engagement.

Another study published in 2002 by the *Journal of Demographics of the Economic Commission for Latin America and the Caribbean* (ECLAC) showed that adolescents living with single mothers in multigenerational households develop "at least as good as, and many times better than, those of adolescents in families with married couples."

---

3. Richard J. Petts, "Single Mothers' Religious Participation and Early Childhood Behavior," *Journal of Marriage and Family*, vol. 74, issue 2, 251–268.

However, there are always exceptions to almost any rule. There are also single mothers who, in one way or another, fail their children. But what I am attempting to show you is that your identity as a mother doesn't stop just because you do not have a husband by your side. In such cases, there is no better ally than God.

LAPAROSCOPY AND HYSTERECTOMY

When I first heard these surgical terms, I had no idea what they meant. I said, "Laparo...what? Hyster...what?"

I had the first surgery, laparoscopic tubal ligation, to tie my fallopian tubes after my third delivery, unaware that I would later need to have the second surgery, a hysterectomy, because fibroids were causing health-related issues in my uterus. A hysterectomy is commonly known as removal of the uterus. The doctor warned me to think about the ramifications because it's an irreversible procedure, but in the end, I had to do it because of my health.

After these surgeries, I experienced psychological repercussions due to natural reactions in my body. I was wired to be a mother, but I had now stripped my body of its inherent function. I had a severe identity crisis in which I inadvertently began to question whether I would be able to perform my role as a mother with ease. By then, my oldest son was not even ten years old.

One night in Costa Rica—more than twenty-five years ago—I was with my husband at an important conference on the subject of the Holy Spirit in the church. I was sitting in the first couple of rows, feeling so uncomfortable that I disliked everything: the speakers, the people, the atmosphere, the message, the music— everything. I suddenly knew I didn't want to be there. No one was doing anything wrong; the problem was me. *I* was the issue. Even though I never reneged against God or my faith at any time, I just wanted to leave there. I told God, "Lord, help me find someone to explain what is happening to me."

As I was about to leave the room, a lady passed by me. I took her by the arm and told her that I needed to get something off my chest. I began to cry with a feeling of despair. I said I was not comfortable there and that something I couldn't understand was happening to me. She looked at me and said, "I am a psychologist." Right then, I began to laugh because I realized that it was God who was sending me an answer through her.

After I was done laughing, I thought she was going to say something like, "C'mon, let's pray," or "You need to repent," or that she was going to minister to me in some other way. Instead, she simply asked me, "You didn't just have surgery to stop having children, did you?" I said, "As a matter of fact, yes," and thought how amazing it was that she would lead off with that.

She said that many times, when doctors explain this type of surgery to women, they overlook the fact that not only is the ability to procreate blocked but also the natural process of ovulation. The situation affects women psychologically and has repercussions on their emotions and even their sexuality.

"You must learn to control these symptoms and not allow them to control you," the psychologist told me. "Keep an eye on how many days affect you the most during the month and manage your feelings beforehand."

It all started with a simple operation, leading me to doubt even essential decisions about my marriage and family. God's wired us, as women, in such a powerful way that when we feel stripped of it, we run the risk of considerably altering our identity.

Life is a miracle, and all women deserve the honor of having children, seeing their children and grandchildren grow, and enjoying that incomparable and indescribable love that only comes with motherhood, which dramatically strengthens our identity.

Dear friend, I am not telling you that you must bear children. In fact, you might decide not to have them altogether, and everyone should respect that. However, one thing you cannot deny is that we were wired and designed for that specific function.

QUESTIONS FOR REFLECTION

1. How ready are you emotionally, physically, and financially to become a mother?

_____

_____

_____

_____

_____

2. Do you have any fears or doubts about becoming a mother?

_____

_____

_____

_____

_____

14

IDENTITY AND CHILDREN

From the moment we started dating, my husband and I talked about the possibility of having several children, although at the time, we didn't exactly agree on how many. I recall that I would have loved to have six, perhaps because I come from a large family, but my husband, who is an only child, perhaps would have settled for two.

In the end, we had three: Carlos Enrique "Cashito," Juan Diego, and Ana Gabriela. We followed the psychologist's recommendation to have no more than three years in between births to avoid a generation gap between them so they could be closer in age. That is why they were born exactly two and a half years apart.

It was only after Ana Gabriela's birth that I began to manifest an identity crisis that would surface at different times, one of which I described in the previous chapter. But after sharing my feelings with other women, I realized that mine was not an isolated incident and that these crises are common among us, generally appearing when we are in the fullness of life.

When we are married and have children, we usually start wondering if we are raising them well or have made the best decision to create a home. If we are single, we begin to wonder if we will ever raise a family or fulfill our personal goals, such as having a career or owning our own home. I associate all of this with what we commonly call a midlife crisis, but I would venture to say that it is more pronounced among women.

One day, I asked myself, "We've got three children—now what?" Although I've always had my husband's unconditional support in every way, both financially and emotionally, I felt very lonely at home with the responsibility of caring for the children when they were little while Cash was going out to preach. I felt lonely without really being isolated because Cash was always watching over everything, even when he was not present. He called us on the phone every day to see how we were doing and was interested in how things were going at home.

During those years, my routine consisted of dropping the children off at school and picking them up at the end of the day, helping them with homework, doing household chores, and carrying out various tasks for my husband's business, such as keeping his appointment book or filing documents. I would do all of this from home, and it was a bit exhausting, so much so that those desires to have six children began to fade and turn into doubts, concerns, and a lack of personal satisfaction with the family I already had.

When I started to feel that *I* was the one with the problem, I asked God in prayer if I should have more children. His answer came in the form of more ministry activities, not only for my husband but also for me and our children as they became older. It was then that I decided to have my fallopian tubes tied because of the fibroid problems I mentioned earlier.

A CONSTANT LEARNING EXPERIENCE

When we were new to parenting, Cash encouraged me to read books about raising children. I came across several interesting titles, such as *How to Develop Your Child's Temperament* by Beverly LaHaye and *Help Me! I'm a Parent* by Dr. Bruce Narramore.

These books and others taught me that I had to get to know each child individually and not expect them to have the same reactions and behaviors. To help me visualize their differences, one day, I imagined what would happen if I gave each of them a chocolate bar that was the same brand and size. Cashito would probably gobble it down quickly and then go out with his friends. Juan Diego would eat the chocolate slowly and ask for another one. Ana Gabriela, on the other hand, would save her chocolate for later.

I also learned different ways of correcting them according to their particular temperaments. While I spanked all three when they misbehaved, Cashito learned best when the punishment included taking away some privileges. On the other hand, Juan Diego was more intimidated by a severe scolding where I made him see the seriousness of his mistake. With Ana Gabriela, an intervention by her father worked better than any punishment I could ever give her. For that reason, both parents must be actively involved in their children's upbringing.

Both parents must be actively involved in their children's upbringing.

As they grew up, I saw myself reflected in some of their good qualities as well as their flaws. I could see characteristics that once influenced my identity now influencing theirs. For example, Ana Gabriela would flare up just as I did when I was a teenager. Cashito would also get angry, but without externalizing it, reminding me of myself as a child. These are just some of the traits that connect me to them. Since I was able to overcome these traits in my own life so as to not affect my identity, I knew they could do the same.

One day, when my oldest son was eight or nine, he did something wrong, and I called him home to correct him. At the time, Cashito was riding his bike with his friends. When I explained what he had done wrong, he leaned over for me to spank him on the buttocks without giving it a second thought.

He told me, "Alright, let's hurry up and spank me and get it over with. Hurry, please."

The punishment didn't bother him! He wanted to keep on biking with his friends. His attitude annoyed me even more, but I did not take it out on him at that moment. Instead, I asked God for wisdom and understanding on how to correct Cashito. That day, I discovered that paddling Cashito was not enough of a punishment; I was going to have to deprive him of the things he enjoyed the most.

While Cashito was more extroverted, Juan Diego was quite the opposite, very melancholy and sentimental. Once, when he was very young, my husband and I found him crying in his room because his shoes did not match his clothes. We patiently explained to him that this was not a reason to cry, and instead of buying him another pair, we encouraged him to wear those shoes, even though he thought they didn't match what he was wearing.

We wanted to show him that there was no real problem with his outfit and that people often have to learn to live with things that they don't consider ideal.

Even as a child, Ana Gabriela was known for having a strong and dominant personality compared to her brothers. From a very young age, she showed excellent negotiating skills that would often enable her to get what she wanted—and she did not take it too well when she didn't. On one occasion, I asked her to pick up a sweater that her brother had inadvertently dropped on the floor, but I never expected her reaction.

"And why do I have to pick it up?" she said. "Let him do it!"

So I told her, "Because he dropped it by accident, and it's a way of serving him."

"Well, no, let him serve me. Why do I have to serve him?" was her final reply.

All of this helped me realize how I could help them. While we each had different ways of reacting to childhood conflict, my husband and I applied the same golden rule that my parents applied with me: we never compared them. We never once said things like, "He's more capable than you," or "Perhaps she'd be better off handling that than you." Although sometimes one of them would complain that I had favorites—which was certainly not the case—I always showed them that I loved them all the same and that there are different ways of giving and receiving love.

Psychologists say there are different types of attachments, including negative ones such as anxious attachment, ambivalent attachment, avoidant attachment, and disordered attachment. However, there is also something known as secure attachment and bonding, which forms when parents are responsive and sensitive, allowing children to develop a healthy self-image and a feeling of trust toward others. Attachment is a natural condition in human beings, whereas codependency is unhealthy.

We all have different ways of loving others, depending on who it is. For example, while Juan Diego will give me a flower, Cashito, with his witty eloquence, makes me laugh. Ana Gabriela, on the other hand, took the role of being an inseparable friend. She always involved me in her activities and accompanied me everywhere. She even encouraged me to go on diets and to the gym with her. Their ways of loving were always different, and I reacted accordingly.

I spent approximately twelve years raising my children while I was totally devoted to my home. It was an extraordinary time in which I was exclusively available to them, and I would not change it for anything. During that period, I was not yet a pastor, nor was I carrying out the ministry I had founded with my husband. Furthermore, it was also a time when Cash and I influenced our children's personalities to help them find their infinite catalyst and define their identity. In short, we showed them the way so that they could see the answer themselves.

By the time they were nine years old, the results of what we had sown in their minds and hearts were starting to show. They were already expressing their own opinions and ideas about money, alcohol, lies, friends, drugs, and sex. I observed how they played, competed, fed themselves, and even the way they put their toys away.

As parents, Cash and I took it upon ourselves to reinforce good Christian habits and values in our children, but at different times in their lives, each of them made a personal decision to accept Jesus's love and forgiveness and serve God. Today, all three are married and work as full-time pastors, but we never imposed this path or any other on them. We simply showed them what we were doing and allowed them to have their own personal encounter with God. This enabled them to find their infinite catalyst, which allowed them to be where they are today.

WHEN OUR FAMILY GREW THROUGH ADOPTION

I do not want to leave out our experience as adoptive parents. Many years ago, one of Cash's cousins had a fatal accident, leaving Andrea, a beautiful six-year-old girl, an orphan. She stayed with her grandmother until she passed away. Andrea was thirteen years old at the time.

We asked our children what they thought of the idea of us adopting Andrea. They all agreed to open the doors of our home and provide her with all of the emotional, academic, and spiritual support she needed so she could develop in life, just as they had. Thus, we took Andrea in as our daughter.

The whole family quickly became very fond of her. Ana Gabriela had no sisters, so when Andrea came into our lives, the two girls became close.

And just like Cashito, Juan Diego, and Ana Gabriela, Andrea also had to mature in her own time. With her, I learned that every child must overcome obstacles that prevent them from growing as people. These issues can include abandonment and abuse as well as overprotection.

Today, Andrea is an adult woman in the prime of her youth. Although she no longer lives with us, we still love her and always look out for her. The twelve years she lived with us also tested my identity as a mother and proved to me that there is no perfect family. Although I was not her biological mother, I believed I could step into that role, which was not possible. In what may have been her own identity crisis, she felt a natural need to reconnect with her origins and search for a sense of belonging that had been stripped away from her during childhood. This was only possible when we were able to release her to do it on her own.

QUESTIONS FOR REFLECTION

1. Do you know each of your children's personality types? Do you respect them and know how to interact with each one as they are?

_____

_____

_____

_____

_____

2. How do you adapt your identity to improve your relationships with your children?

_____

_____

_____

_____

_____

15

WHY DO I SERVE GOD AND PEOPLE?

Wherever I preach the Word of God, people always ask me the same questions. One of them is, "Can a woman head a Christian ministry?" My answer has always been the same: "Of course she can. Why shouldn't she?"

But rather than being in charge, I see Christian ministry more as a matter of service. Pastoring a congregation is not the only way to serve God and people, nor is it the easiest or the most inspiring. I would dare to say that it is one of the most likely to provoke an identity crisis, which all religious leaders have faced at least once in their ministry.

Pastoring a congregation
is not the only way we can
serve God and people.

Another question I get is, "Why should I serve?" The main reason to serve would have to be out of love. However, serving in ministry also brings a guaranteed blessing. God will never stand idly by in the face of our good intentions to help people.

Others ask me how they can serve. A couple of years ago, I had the opportunity to write the commentary for the book *21 Wonderful Gifts from God* by Chiqui Corzo. In it, the author reorders and classifies the gifts the Lord gives to people according to the books of Corinthians, Ephesians, and Romans. She explains and analyzes the features of each one, providing biblical and practical everyday situations with them.

God gave us gifts and talents to serve others. In Fraternidad Cristiana de Guatemala, our mother church—the first one Cash and I attended that formed us and wherein we took our first steps of faith—I was allowed to serve in different areas.

Initially, I started serving in the church during the Sunday services by taking care of children, from newborns to pre-teens. I did this for many years and continued to do so when Casa de Dios was founded. Something I'll never forget was when my oldest son first said "mama" to me in the Sunday school nursery while I was caring for other babies.

I also had the opportunity to be a part of the church choir. I have always loved to sing and worship God. Although I don't have the voice of a soloist, God granted me the opportunity to record a cassette of praise songs as a background singer, together with other vocalists.

In addition, I was a greeter at the temple doors and coordinated youth groups with my husband, helping to strengthen their spiritual growth.

My point is this: there are many different ways to serve. You just have to take one step forward and offer your gifts and talents. You don't have to be a preacher or an evangelist to please God with your service.

The first time I stepped onto a pulpit as a pastor, I had already served in other areas for about twenty years. In fact, while my husband had already been the senior pastor of Casa de Dios for several years, I was still serving in Sunday school. Serving is part of our DNA as a church, not only as Christians but also as an institution that cares for people's emotional and spiritual well-being. Besides, serving also gives us an identity as children of God and coheirs with Jesus.

AS A PASTOR

I want to clarify something for women called to serve God whose husbands have been called to the ministry. You are not obligated to start functioning as a female pastor! The first operational gift we have is to serve God. You can help and contribute to many areas of ministry while raising your children, tending to your home, and conscientiously and lovingly carrying out your family ministry. I evolved in my service to God to become the pastor I am today.

Casa de Dios was founded as a church in the mid-1990s, but I did not step onto a pulpit as a preacher until 2001. Why not earlier? Because I still had a lot of work to do as a mom: finishing raising my children, helping them in their studies, playing sports, and developing in life. When I got married, never once did it cross my mind to be a leader with Cash in a Christian ministry of international influence such as Casa de Dios.

I can't deny that the situation also affected my identity and filled me with recurring doubts throughout the years. Many times,

I know that God is just as
pleased to see me in a pulpit
now as He was to see me
taking care of babies many
years ago.

I thought, *People come to me for advice and ministry, but who is looking out for me?* Women would ask me to intercede for them before God to help them fulfill their dreams, but I wondered, *What about my dreams and what I wanted in life when I was young?*

As I look back, I realize that all this time as a pastor and preacher has been very rewarding because it has allowed me to get close to people and know firsthand how they think and how God has worked in their lives. While it is true that preaching has been a great blessing, this calling is also directly related to the satisfaction of serving.

MARRIED TO A PUBLIC FIGURE

Some people have said to me, "Pastor, you're so blessed with the husband God gave you." And yes, it's true. I am blessed because the Lord brought us together, and we love each other, get along well, and above all, we greatly respect each other, which has been a two-way street since the beginning.

I'm also asked, "How do you feel about being married to a well-known person?" My reply is that I feel very blessed, but I never express my concerns because, after all, Cash is always exposed.

When we met, he was not a public figure; however, he was a handsome, hardworking, and energetic young man, an intelligent athlete and leader who knew very well what he wanted to do in life and that was to serve God. I thank the Lord that He allowed us to mature, step by step, in each stage of our lives. After all, if I had known Cash as a high-profile person, I would have probably fled from any relationship with him.

However, it doesn't affect me now. Although I have gone through an identity crisis in my marriage, it has been more about doubts with my child-rearing abilities, never about being overshadowed by my husband. I know that God is just as pleased to see me in a pulpit now as He was to see me taking care of babies many years ago, for everything that adds to His kingdom is readily welcome.

EXPANDING GOD'S KINGDOM

My husband often says, "Those whom God uses and anoints with His Spirit are the ones He gives more work and responsibility to." Due to life circumstances, the day came when we had to make changes in how we served God and answered His call. We stopped being the youth coordinators at the church we were attending and opened a new ministry to continue expanding His kingdom.

Before this happened, however, we asked Jorge Lopez, our senior pastor at Fraternidad Cristiana church, for advice. He prayed for us, wishing us the best and trusting that we would carry out this new stage in our life with effort and ease.

So it was that after eleven years of continual service in our mother church, we moved to a sector on the outskirts of Guatemala City, where there were no churches at the time. My husband began preaching the Word in the living room of the home of some dear friends of ours, and it wasn't many weeks before we outgrew the house and had to move to a lot in the back.

Since then, our church growth has been supernatural. One by one, warehouses, hotel ballrooms, and temples have become too small for the number of people who attend Casa de Dios, motivating us to grow in faith even more.

The book *To the Architect and Maker of the Universe* analyzes the architectural history of our temples and the beginnings of Casa de Dios as a church. Throughout these years, beyond bringing people to the feet of Christ, our work has been to motivate them to create networks and friendship groups following our Lord and Savior's example. Based on the Scriptures found in Matthew 28:19 and John 15:13, our vision statement says:

> Go out and make disciples of all Guatemalans,
>
> Teaching them what Jesus commanded through friendship groups,
>
> Where we are taught to lay down our life for our friends.

I can attest that Casa de Dios would not exist today were it not for our members' commitment to serve others and the friendship groups that have strengthened and given it an identity as a church. I feel very fortunate to serve in a Christian ministry that is based on friendship.

QUESTIONS FOR REFLECTION

1. In what areas of ministry do you feel called to serve God?

_____

_____

_____

_____

_____

2. How do you connect your call to your identity?

_____

_____

_____

_____

_____

16

THE BLESSING OF INTERCEDING

Prayer is the simplest and most straightforward way to talk to God, but intercession goes beyond that because it reveals our love for others. A prayer of intercession is no more than one in which we ask the Lord to heal someone else's physical, emotional, or spiritual afflictions.

JESUS: THE GREAT INTERCESSOR

Jesus is the perfect example of an intercessor. He did not come to heal those who were whole but those who were sick. He did not come to save the righteous but sinners. That is why Christians preach about the Savior, the One who loves and delivers us from eternal death if we trust in Him.

To God, I am no more or less special than Anna, Victor, or anyone else whose testimonies I have shared in this book. We are all sinners and are under construction, meaning that our identity is shaped from before our birth until the last day of our lives. Therefore, we must accept each other for who we are and who we choose to be, interceding for one another before the Father.

Since 2004, I have been directing the Intercession Ministry at Casa de Dios. We train and equip intercessors to pray for the salvation of others, but we also pray for healing for the physical and emotional ailments people suffer in their journey through this world. I desire that every person come to know Christ and intercede for the welfare of other sinners who do not yet know Him. Although God hates sin, He loves the sinner because we are all His children.

THE CHURCH'S CALL TO INTERCEDE

The church was established by God on earth not to judge or condemn but to facilitate the reconciliation of people to His love.

Now all things are of God, who has reconciled us to Himself through Jesus Christ, and has given us the ministry of reconciliation, that is, that God was in Christ reconciling the world to Himself, not imputing their trespasses to them, and has committed to us the word of reconciliation.

(2 Corinthians 5:18–19)

The Christian church should never reject sinners but instead welcome them so they may come to know the Lord's loving-kindness. The church should instruct them in the Word of God in order for

The church was established
by God not to judge or
condemn but to facilitate
the reconciliation of people
to His love.

them to make the best decisions for their lives. And it must speak to them of the marvelous gift of salvation and reiterate in a thousand and one ways that Jesus also paid the price for their sins.

Let us follow Christ's lead and never discriminate against anyone for any reason whatsoever. God has entrusted us with the care of all, as we urge them to turn away from their vain manner of living without ever holding back His love for them. Galatians 6:1–2 says, "*Brethren, if a man is overtaken in any trespass, you who are spiritual restore such a one in a spirit of gentleness, considering yourself lest you also be tempted. Bear one another's burdens, and so fulfill the law of Christ.*"

As a senior pastor of Casa de Dios and founder of the Intercessory Ministry, I have always ensured that our prayers of intercession are motivated by the right reasons: for the care and welfare of others. In our prayers, we also ask for the physical healing of atheists, the emotional well-being of people who despise us, the understanding of people of other religions who do not believe in Jesus, and wisdom in those who govern us, whether they do it well or not.

Intercession is all a matter of loving others and trusting that God can change their lives for the better.

QUESTIONS FOR REFLECTION

1. Does your church practice the habit of interceding for others?

    _____

    _____

    _____

    _____

    _____

2. When was the last time you interceded before the Lord for someone?

    _____

    _____

    _____

    _____

    _____

EPILOGUE:
OUR INFINITE CATALYST
KNOWN AS GOD

My parents baptized my siblings and me according to the rules of the Catholic Church, so I know that they at least believed in God. However, we hardly ever attended Mass, and we never went through the Catholic sacraments that other children did.

The first real encounter I recall having with God was when I was nine years old. Without even knowing what a boyfriend was, I asked God that if I ever had a boyfriend that he would see me as pretty, love me, and be wholly interested in me.

This intimate encounter with the Lord has happened several times throughout my lifetime, in good times and bad times. He's been there when I've gone through identity crises and when I've enjoyed greater self-esteem and security. He's been there when I've thanked Him for His infinite love, and when I rejected the plans He had for me because I did not understand them at the time.

Years after that first childhood prayer, God has manifested Himself time and time again with greater strength. Dinora Jacobs, my childhood friend in Retalhuleu, continued to be my friend during my teenage years when we moved back to Guatemala City. She always listened to me when there were problems at home and when I needed someone to talk to, so I often ran to her for comfort. Today I see Dinora as an example of friends in every stage of life who mark us forever. And God has blessed me with many friends like her, each one important to me.

Something I will never forget is the peace and harmony I always felt at Dinora's home when I was growing up. There was something different, a feeling of happiness that I could not explain and could not feel in my own house, despite living next door. It wasn't long before I realized that what she had in her home and what was missing from mine was God. I wanted that feeling of being close to God in my own life.

When we were young, Dinora spent a lot of time inviting me to a seven-day youth camp. She was so insistent that one day, she finally convinced me. I had just turned fifteen, and my heart was once again challenged as I experienced an intense encounter with the Lord. During the retreat, I recognized for the first time that we are all sinners and need salvation. And so following an invitation to receive Jesus, I decided to pray that simple yet powerful prayer that gives us our identity in God.

If you confess with your mouth the Lord Jesus and believe in your heart that God has raised Him from the dead, you will be saved. For with the heart one believes unto righteousness, and with the mouth confession is made unto salvation.

(Romans 10:9–10)

Since then, my life has changed. God became my infinite catalyst and has always been present.

That is not to say that my life has been perfect. In fact, when I thought those initial experiences with God were already a thing of the past, I felt no qualms about complaining to Him when my brother Calin passed away. I was full of resentment and hungry for revenge, asking Him, "Why did you take him and not someone else?" But I also gave God infinite thanks when He saved my daughter Ana Gabriela and me after going through a very complicated delivery during her birth.

Later, there was a moment when I also doubted whether I had made the best decision to marry under His covenant. Still, today I continue to thank Him for the love miracles that He works in people around me like Anna, Victor, and Julia. It constantly confirms that nothing is impossible for Him.

My point is that, in one way or another, God's presence has always been constant in my life, even when I had a wrong notion of Him and doubted His good plans for my life. He has become my infinite catalyst, the reason why I get up every day.

Today, I can assure you that my identity is strengthened in God. I have no doubt that He is not only my infinite catalyst but He can also be yours and the infinite catalyst of any person who seeks a fulfilling life. And I am not only referring to eternity but a fulfilling life here on the earth as well.

No matter your age, it is never too late for you to experience the infinite catalyst known as God.

God has determined my identity as a daughter who, despite being imperfect, will never feel abandoned, no matter how much the world confuses me with new trends and fashions.

Thanks to Him, I now know that I am someone not only because of my qualities and flaws but also because nothing happens by chance. His love defines me and is present in my essential decisions and even in my oversights.

With this book, I invite you to not only discover your true identity as part of this world but also to explore the possibility of making God the infinite catalyst of your life too. Even if you're at odds with Him right now, or you do not understand Him or His ways of working in you, let me tell you that you don't need to understand Him to realize that He loves you.

In fact, something as simple as our freedom to choose whether to love God or not is nothing more than a sign of His infinite goodness.

Woman, no matter your age, it is never too late for you to experience the infinite catalyst known as God. That's not to say that your life will be perfect after you do so and accept Christ as your Savior—for even as you've noticed throughout the pages of this book, my life has never been perfect despite His presence. But what I can assure you is that He will give you a purpose and reason for being every single day, every single hour, minute, and second of your life.

More than an infinite catalyst, God is a universal catalyst because He is within everyone's reach. He is the reason why my life was forever transformed, just as God changed the lives of Anna, Victor, Julia, and many other people I have had the joy of knowing since my initial encounter with God at the age of nine.

BALANCING QUESTIONNAIRE

Asking ourselves questions leads us to a state of reflection, inspiration, and motivation. It also helps us make decisions that affect our way of thinking and living for the better. The idea is to get to know ourselves better and never allow life to continue without enjoying what we do and maintaining a clear purpose. Questioning ourselves and giving ourselves honest and objective answers will also help us find meaning in the events of our lives.

Likewise, when we externalize our doubts, we bring situations in our subconscious to light that we have not explored or simply have not appropriately examined in our lives. For example, it could be an unexpressed frustration at the time of an argument or a disagreement with someone else. Perhaps many things would have been different if we had expressed what we were feeling at the time.

I can assure you that you will be able to mature, evolve, and grow to the extent that you begin to ask yourself questions, analyze yourself, and question your actions. However, to engage in genuine transformation, each question must be paired with a transparent and honest answer to yourself. Moreover, the short, medium, and long-term results will make you feel fulfilled and committed to your Creator.

Often, when in doubt, we immediately turn to the Scriptures to know what we should do. However, I would like to urge you to understand the difference between doing what must be done—the instructions we find in God's Word—and what we want to do. To see results in our lives, knowing the former is not enough, but you must also discover the latter.

So, if the answer to what we must do is in the Bible, I invite you to consider what it is that you want to do. What changes do you need to want to do what you must do—and enjoy it?

That is why I would like to suggest a series of questions that will challenge you and help you question yourself. I clarify that these are not necessarily the only questions, but every time you have doubts about who you are or where you are going in life, you should start off by asking them.

Use a notebook to do this exercise once a month.

On one page of the notebook, write the date and copy these ten questions, with enough space to answer:

1. Who am I?

2. Why am I in this world?

3. Why do I do what I do every day?

4. Do I have a life purpose? If yes, to what extent am I committed to that life goal?

5. What is my greatest motivation today?

6. What is my greatest motivation in life?

7. In what areas of my life do I feel dissatisfied?

8. What do I want to do?

9. What must I do? (If you are in doubt, you can prayerfully turn to the Scriptures to find the answer.)

10. What do I need to do to balance what I want to do and what I must do?

Except for question nine—which you may wish to search the Bible and pray about—answer each question as honestly as possible with the first thing that pops into your heart. Do not answer with what your mind or intelligence tells you is correct. Answering all ten questions will provide you with an overview of your identity, where you come from, and where you are headed in life.

Your answer for question ten should lead you to make decisions that positively impact your life.

Repeat this questionnaire in the same notebook and on the same calendar date one month later. For example, if you first answered these questions on May 27, do so again on June 27 and so on, indefinitely.

Go over your answers every month and compare them with the previous month's answers. Write your progress down and share it with the people you love the most.

ABOUT THE AUTHOR

Pastor Sonia Luna is known for her faith and simplicity of heart. She is a woman who walks in the presence of the Holy Spirit. Her teachings are known for containing sharp revelations of the Word of God and characterized by her genuine and pleasant way of sharing them.

She received the Lord at the age of seventeen on a Christian retreat. Since then, she has remained steadfast in His ways, passionately serving Him. She started in the worship ministry and was a member of the deacon ministry in her church. She later went on to found Casa de Dios' children's and youth ministries, known as Iglekids.

The daughter of an airline pilot and an elementary school teacher, she grew up in a home with five siblings. The year she gave her heart to God, she graduated as a bilingual executive secretary in Guatemala. In addition, she studied at Cosecha al Mundo, an international training and equipping ministry, obtaining her degree as a reverend.

At a very young age, she met Cash Luna, with whom she would share the rest of her life. She married at the age of nineteen and has three children: Carlos Enrique, Juan Diego, and Ana Gabriela. All three have formed their own families and work full-time in the ministry, serving the Lord.

Sonia and Cash Luna immediately obeyed God's call on their lives. Under the Holy Spirit's anointing, they began to hold meetings to share the Word of God with a small group in the home of one of the three families who started attending. Thus, Casa de Dios was born. From the very beginning, Sonia unconditionally and actively supported her husband, even though doing so meant leaving aside a professional and business life.

Sonia directs Casa de Dios' intercessory ministry, promoting prayer and intercession and training people with biblical principles to stand in the gap for their families, the church, and the nation. She leads the team that tends to the prayer requests the ministry receives from all over Latin America.

She shares the Word through various women's conferences and ministries. She has contributed to reading materials such as *21 Wonderful Gifts from God* and the *Intercession Manual*, among others. She also shares her personal experiences in her blog at www.sonialuna.org, where she provides guidance in the areas of prayer, fasting, and personal and spiritual growth.

The Association of Evangelical Ministers of Guatemala has honored Sonia for her ministerial career. Her presence on various social networks, where she shares messages of faith and hope, has established her as an influential woman, along with national media personalities.

Sonia's greatest heartfelt desire is to serve the Lord in gratitude for His goodness. She feels infinitely blessed that God has honored her as a woman, wife, mother, grandmother, and influential leader.

To learn more about Sonia Luna, visit www.sonialuna.org.

Facebook: /psonialuna

Instagram: @pastorasonialuna

Twitter: @PSonialuna

YouTube: /pastorasonialuna

Phone: PBX: (502) 6679-1919